RETRO STUD

MUSCLE MOVIE POSTERS FROM AROUND THE WORLD

Written by

DAVID CHAPMAN

COLLECTORS PRESS

PORTLAND, OREGON

Copyright © 2002 Collectors Press, Inc.

Library of Congress Cataloging-in-Publication Data

Chapman, David.
Retro stud : muscle movie posters from around the
world / by David Chapman.
    p. cm.
  ISBN 1-888054-69-7 (alk. paper)
  1. Film posters—Catalogs. 2. Peplum films—
Posters—Catalogs. I. Title.
  PN1995.9.P5 C49 2002
  016.79143'75–dc21

                              2002005730

Design: Trina Stahl, Evan Holt
Editor: Ann Granning Bennett

Printed in China
First American edition
9 8 7 6 5 4 3 2 1

Collectors Press books are available at special discounts
for bulk purchases, premiums, and promotions. Special
editions, including personalized inserts or covers, and
corporate logos, can be printed in quantity for special
purposes. For further information contact: Special Sales,
Collectors Press, Inc.,
P.O. Box 230986, Portland, OR 97281.
Toll-free: 1-800-423-1848

For a free catalog write: Collectors Press, Inc., P.O. Box
230986, Portland, OR 97281. Toll-free: 1-800-423-1848
or visit our website at: www.collectorspress.com

DEDICATION

To David Berryman. This book wouldn't exist without him.

ACKNOWLEDGMENTS

Many kind people have helped me put this book together. Among
them are George and Caroline Coune, Ileana Romanazzi, and Patrick
Giraud. Many thanks also to Orhan Kemal Koçak who not only helped
me acquire many posters but also translated the Turkish titles. All of
these dealers in vintage movie posters have shown a great degree of
generosity, friendship and patience with me.

CONTENTS

RETRO STUD

MUSCLE MOVIE POSTERS FROM AROUND THE WORLD

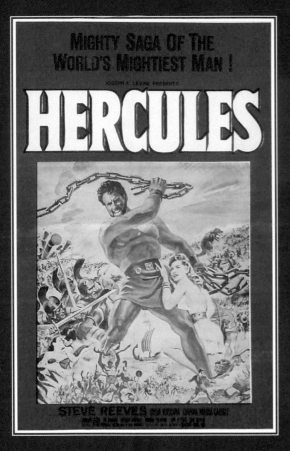

MIGHTY SAGA OF THE WORLD'S MIGHTIEST MAN !

JOSEPH E. LEVINE PRESENTS

HERCULES

STEVE REEVES

Publicity flier sent to theater operators in the media blitz preceding the release of *Hercules*, 1959.

Posters that teem with heroes in rippling muscles and skimpy loincloths, frail beauties in diaphanous gowns, pointy-bearded tyrants, and evil queens with heavy makeup and beehive hairdos—these were all classic lures that were used to tempt patrons into theaters to see the sword-and-sandal movies of the 1960s. The combination of rippling sinews, bold action, and the hint of possible sex were all used shamelessly by the promoters of muscle movies. As a result of these advertisements, people throughout the world flocked to such films.

Known as gladiator movies in America, a more exact and respectful name for these movies is peplum films. In the mid-1970s French critics coined this term, which refers to the peplus or short, pleated skirt worn by many of the Classical-era heroes. A peplum film gradually came to mean any movie set in ancient times featuring a muscular, scantily-clad hero[1].

From the late 1950s and continuing for more than a decade, Italian and Eastern European studios churned out a vast number of films in a remarkably short period. Hercules and his equally beefy successors quickly charged onto the screens of the world righting wrongs, slaying enemies, and destroying marble palaces. Despite the

resulting mayhem, moviegoers around the globe couldn't have been happier. As popular as they were, these films could never have achieved the success that they did without the work of scores of marketing people, and the labors of these anonymous ad men were in many respects even more impressive than the feats of the muscular heroes whom they were touting.

The story of how *Hercules* (1957), an obscure Italian costume adventure was transformed into box office gold through the alchemy of Hollywood marketing is one that has attained fabulous proportions in the annals of advertising. Producer-director Pietro Francisi was searching desperately for a lead in a film that was about to be shot called *Le Fattiche di Ercole* [*The Labors of Hercules*], but no one had appeared who had the right combination of muscularity and drop-dead good looks —acting skill was of minimal importance because like all Italian films of the time, it was to be dubbed. At this fortuitous moment, the producer's thirteen year-old daughter supposedly rushed home and told her astonished papa about a gorgeous hunk of man that she had just seen in the MGM musical, *Athena* (1956)[2]. The

ABOVE: French shoppers on the Champs Élysées were regaled by this large poster of Steve Reeves in *Hercules*. This photo was taken shortly after the film's European release in 1957.

man's name was Steve Reeves, and the daughter was certain that she had found the perfect actor to play the part of Hercules in her father's movie. After screening the film, Francisi agreed and wired Reeves to come to Rome and make the film.

After achieving a moderate success in Europe, the movie came to the attention of producer Joseph E. Levine, a former garment worker who had learned early the lesson of buy cheap and sell dear. After entering the business of film distribution, Levine had picked up several foreign-made movies and presented them to the lucrative American market with a combination of savvy and hype that made hits out of many of them. When Levine saw *Le Fattiche di Ercole*, he knew at once that mid-century Americans could be made to love it if he promoted the movie carefully. Following his hunch, the producer purchased the film rights for a paltry $120,000 and then convinced Warner Brothers that they should spend many times that amount to lure the public into theaters to view the unimpressive epic.

Levine's marketing genius was revealed in the way the movie

ABOVE: Reg Park follows the first rule of all peplum films: when in doubt, throw something.

OPPOSITE: *Hercules Attacks.* (Great Britain)

ABOVE: Steve Reeves and the canny producer, Joseph E. Levine, bask in Italian sunshine on the set of *Hercules Unchained*, 1959.

was released and publicized. Instead of following the usual methods of releasing a film in those days, Levine pioneered saturation booking. This meant that he rejected the system of issuing films in exclusive engagements, followed by slowly releasing them into neighborhood theaters. Under Levine's new system, films played in as many theaters as possible all at once. The idea was to inundate the public with the films rather than teasing average moviegoers with releases in exclusive venues only.

In order for this system to work, massive publicity campaigns had to blanket the continent. This is where Levine's real creativity came in.

At the beginning of the campaign, Levine threw an elaborate luncheon for a thousand people at the Waldorf-Astoria Hotel in Manhattan. At this "herculean explodation," so called because, "we are going to explode HERCULES throughout the nation this summer," guests received fancy press kits, posters, and other marketing accessories. Those who attended could marvel at the colorful posters, gaudy banners, and a two-story cardboard cutout of Reeves in leopard skin and sandals, as they listened to singer-band leader Vaughn Monroe croon the theme from *Hercules*.

Soon, four-color, full-page ads began to appear in *Life*, *Look*, *Parade* and just about every other major middle-to-lowbrow magazine in the country. But that was not all. Thirty- and sixty-second television spots and posters appeared not just in theater lobbies, but all over town on every spare wall and telephone pole. Reeves' handsome face and muscular physique was omnipresent.

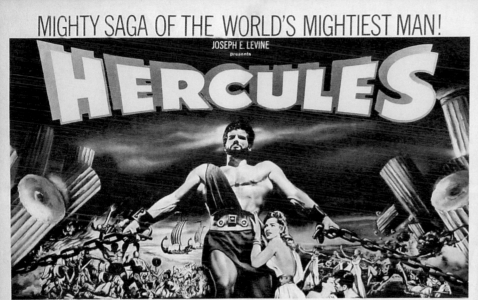

ABOVE: *Hercules.* Half-sheet 1957. (U.S.A.)

ABOVE RIGHT: *Hercules against Rome.* One-sheet 1965. (U.S.A.)

RIGHT: *Hercules vs. the Vampires.* Small one-sheet. An atypical example of French poster design

because of its use of multiple scenes. It is consequently less effective than others.

2,000 Years Back To The Age Of Orgy!

The Invincible Gladiator

SEE! Death-Duel in the Arena!
SEE! Slaughter of the Innocents!
SEE! Revolt of the Gladiators!

starring RICHARD HARRISON / ISABELLE COREY

A Seven Arts Release

LEFT: *The Invincible Hercules.* Peplum's favorite pose
realized brilliantly by Dan Vadis and the artist of this minor
masterpiece. (BELGIUM)

ABOVE: *Hercules against the Sons of the Sun.* (SPAIN)

RIGHT: *The Invincible Gladiator.* One-sheet 1961. (U.S.A.)

Clearly, the wily publicist was targeting his campaign on the American male. Full-page advertisements appeared in 132 magazines. Notices for the hunky movie star showed up in just about every national men's periodical, and the detective and true-crime mags like *Front Page, Detective,* and *Official Detective Stories* were saturated with them. In order to get the men's sons hyped, Dell Comics quickly produced a comic-book version of the film, and a whole new audience was attracted to the film. Clearly, Levine was trying to tap into the male market in a big way. The pudgy producer realized at once that other out-of-shape, postwar males all across North America would respond in a big way to the handsome, muscular, prize-winning athlete who starred in this extravaganza.

The result of this media blitz was just as Levine had foreseen: the movie became an instant success. *Hercules* was seen by an estimated 24 million people, earning a total of $18 million[3]. It was so successful, in fact, that Reeves was soon back in Italy making a sequel, and Italian producers were searching for other well-built American bodybuilders to star in the knockoffs that were quickly in the works. Nearly a decade passed before the resulting fascination with muscular, semi-naked heroes had run its course. But in the splash created by these stories, many secret sensations and unspoken desires washed up on the shores of modern masculinity itself. Levine and others must also have known that posters featuring the sexy bodybuilders in skimpy costumes and bulging muscles were tickling other deeper feelings in the movie-going public.

Italy, the birthplace of the sword-and-sandal film, had been producing epics of this sort for as long as they had a movie industry. There had been earlier stage spectacles like *Ben Hur* and even a 1912 movie version of *Quo Vadis*, but no real beefcake star had emerged from these extravaganzas. All that changed when a burly bodybuilder named Bartolomeo Pagano (1878–1947) was cast as "Maciste," a Nubian slave in the early Italian cast-of-thousands epic, *Cabiria* (1914). His muscular body was darkened with makeup, and his character was at first merely a powerful, playful, and steadfast sidekick, but he ended up stealing the show from the other players. Pagano's persona became so successful that after the initial filming, he was approached by other producers who wanted to expand on his original character. Eventually the actor legally changed his name to that of the character he played in *Cabiria*; from that time forward he was known as Maciste.

Pagano created the character that would later be transformed

OPPOSITE: Steve Reeves displays his pectoral splendor in this publicity still from *Hercules*.

ABOVE RIGHT: *Hercules* Dell comic book, 1959. LEFT: *Hercules Unchained* Dell comic book, 1960.

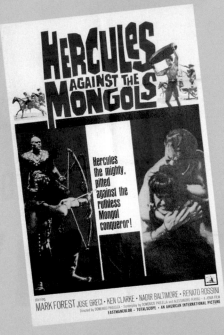

TOP LEFT: *Hercules and the Pirates.* One-sheet 1960. (U.S.A.)

LEFT: *Hercules against the Mongols.* One-sheet 1964. (U.S.A.)

ABOVE: *Hercules in the Haunted World.* Half-sheet.

1962. (U.S.A.) The star of this production, Reg Park was a

well-known bodybuilder.

OPPOSITE: *The Rebel Gladiators.* (Great Britain)

into the hero of a hundred other such films, some (but not all) set in a vaguely Greco-Roman past. Whether he was called Goliath, Ursus, Samson, Hercules, or even Maciste, the hero is the same beefy warrior who fights injustice, villains, and gruesome monsters. Each of these characters is based on the loveable hunk who first made his appearance in 1914. Even in the beginning, poster artists were no fools; they recognized in Maciste an unforgettable character, and the best posters always featured Pagano's massive and shirtless form. Eventually, he went on to make more than twenty-five films playing the gentle and likeable giant, and he thereby engraved in the Italian psyche the memory of his strong and benevolent character[4]. When Italian directors looked for a suitable model for the protagonists of their gladiator movies in the mid-twentieth century, they did not have to search far; they had a ready-made pattern in the person of Maciste[5].

Gladiator movies thus had their beginnings in the earliest days of the European film industry, but then these films died out as they were replaced by Fascist propaganda or lightweight drawing room dramas (called in Italy "white telephone films" because of this symbol of luxury and style). When, after World War II, Italians searched for other ways of diverting themselves, directors like Pietro Francisi looked to the nation's classical past rather than its gritty present, and the strongman movie phenomenon was off and running again.

TOP LEFT: *Quo Vadis* Argentine. One-sheet 1951. BOTTOM LEFT: Bartolomeo Pagano, the man who began the first peplum craze with his role as Maciste in the 1914 epic *Cabiria*. OPPOSITE: *Cabiria.* Artist: A. Vassallo, 1914. The shirtless Maciste stands at the far right.

GABRIELE D'ANNUNZIO
CABIRIA
ITALA FILM - TORINO

Hercules and his brothers were in the cinemas again, but this begs the question of why they became so spectacularly popular in the early 1960s. What messages did these films communicate that endeared them so to popular audiences? How did these messages lure viewers into theaters? Since the sword-and-sandal film was a truly international phenomenon, the same movies were shown in Thailand as well as Toledo, but how did savvy marketers convince such diverse audiences to spend ninety minutes in a dark room as they watched the stories unfold?

The posters and other publicity tools reveal a remarkable variety of appeals and allures. Each nation in which these films were shown wisely tuned its posters to local tastes. Thus, the French and Italians tended to take one dramatic scene from the drama and make it the focus of the poster: minimum text and maximum image. The name of the film is presented in large but unobtrusive lettering, and

LEFT: Bartolomeo Pagano as Maciste in *Cabiria*, 1914.

The strongman flexes his muscles as he attempts to escape Carthaginian chains.

the names of the stars appear in even smaller point sizes. Clearly, these audiences were more interested in the action than the players. Another distinguishing element of the peplum posters of France and Italy is the importance placed on the muscular male physique. Masculine torsos, nude and straining with effort, are at the heart of the message here.

The French (as they usually do) tend to take both film and posters much more seriously than Anglo-American critics. J.M. Monnier, spokesman for an organization of movie poster makers, announced in 1946: "It is a very difficult task to embody the subject of a film which lasts an hour and a half and which is often taken from a novel of three hundred pages on a sheet of paper of a few meters square. This task is made even more difficult by the innumerable constraints which paralyze the artist's inspiration. The movie poster must be popular, that is to say understandable by everyone; it must suggest a simplified synthesis of the subject. It must be pleasing to the eye by its harmonious choice of colors and designed so as to attract attention. At all costs, the artist must respect the striking resemblance of well-known actors whose presence in the film is of the utmost commercial importance, and to avoid shapes that are too simplified or a style that is so abstract that only an artistic minority will understand it. Cinema is a popular art, and the poster designer must conform to it[6]."

RIGHT: *Maciste and the Queen of Samar*, locandina. A masterpiece of monochrome, this locandina shows that adventure did not have to be expressed in vibrant colors. (ITALY)

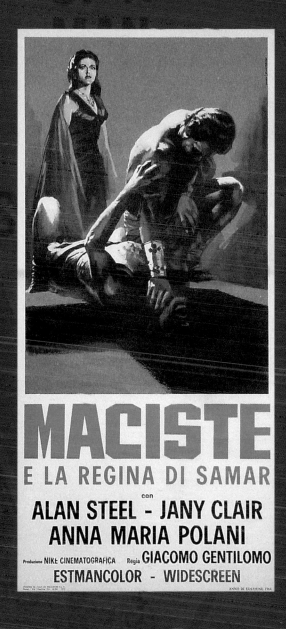

MACISTE
E LA REGINA DI SAMAR
con
ALAN STEEL - JANY CLAIR
ANNA MARIA POLANI
Produzione NIKE CINEMATOGRAFICA   Regia GIACOMO GENTILOMO
ESTMANCOLOR - WIDESCREEN

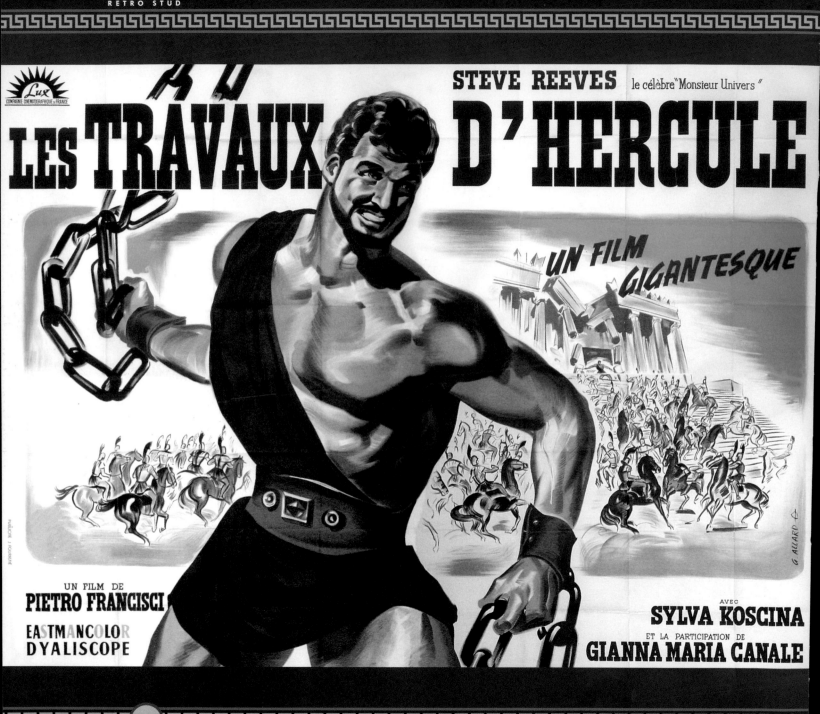

One of the finest French artists to design peplum posters was Claude Belinsky. His distinctive style and brilliant ability to capture the single, defining moment of the film is unsurpassed. Although he designed posters for a variety of genres, Belinsky felt completely at home with the exotic locales and anatomical representations of this movie type. Monnier's description of the poster designer's art seems to describe Belinsky exactly. His ability to distill a convoluted plot into a single image and his talent at conveying the excitement of these adventure films is of the highest quality. The French designer also worked in the stone lithographic method, and he was a genius at using the bright colors that are built up on the page to make the greatest possible impact on the viewer. Other French and Italian poster designers did excellent work, but none were as consistently successful as Claude Belinsky.

French and Italian posters were colorful and sophisticated, but North Americans took a different tack when they designed posters advertising sword-and-sandal films. Words are just as important to Americans as pictures (at least in their movie posters), and these films were promoted with cluttered designs and breathless prose. It is as if Americans were incapable of "reading" the illustrations in order to get a feel for the movie. They had to be told in no uncertain

TOP RIGHT: *The Terror of the Gladiators*. Small one-sheet. The bold, upward slant of Gordon Scott's muscular arm conveys the right amount of motion and tension to make this a masterpiece. (FRANCE)

RIGHT: *The Battle of Corinth*. Large one-sheet. Artist, Claude Belinsky. (FRANCE)

OPPOSITE: *The Labors of Hercules*. Four-sheet. This huge and effective poster was big enough to cover an entire wall. (FRANCE)

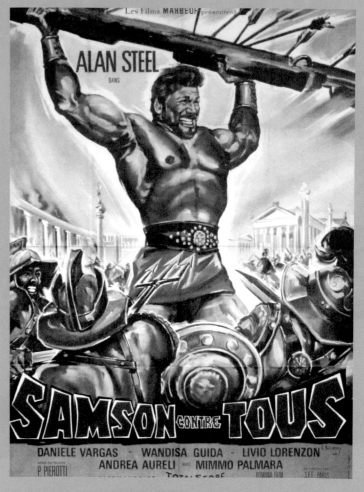

ABOVE: *Maciste vs. the Cyclops*. Large one-sheet. Artist, Claude Belinsky. Chelo Alonso's sultry features float in the corner while Mitchell Gordon's superb physique is shown in a common peplum stunt: the hero is pulled apart by chains. This time it's over a pit of hungry carnivores. (FRANCE) RIGHT: *Samson vs. All*. Large one-sheet. Artist, Claude Belinsky. A particularly powerful design showing Alan Steel fighting off a crowd of gladiators. (FRANCE)

terms what the film was about, who starred in it, and what they could expect. "The Wonder Film of the Year!", "The Most Murderous Massacre of all time!", "It is beyond belief!", "Never Before on the screen! The mightiest of them all!", the posters shouted in all-cap block letters. The credulous viewers were constantly being invited to SEE this, that, or the other wonder of nature. In the poster to *Goliath and the Vampires,* for instance, we are invited to "See the revolt of the faceless humanoids! See the holocaust in the cave of fire! See the torture chamber of the blue men! . . ."

But U.S. posters almost always hinted at something more; something a little more thrilling than even adventure sequences could offer. A sexually suggestive tagline meant to titillate prospective viewers appeared in nearly every American peplum poster. Prospective movie-goers are promised "A surging spectacle of savagery and sex!" on the poster for the Steve Reeves vehicle, *The Trojan Horse,* and in *Goliath and the Barbarians,* viewers are told, "A thousand and one women dream of his embrace." In the poster for *Atlas,* director Roger Corman, America's greatest sleazemeister, tells us that his main character is "feared by every man—desired by every woman," and to confirm his potency, a diaphanously garbed wench grabs Atlas's thigh as she holds an upturned sword suggestively at the strongman's crotch. Even a casual study of the posters reveals a wealth of phallic symbols, from swords, tridents, and spears to uprooted pillars and writhing reptiles.

Often there is a soupçon of sado-masochism implied in the wording on the posters. For example, in the advertisement for *Goliath*

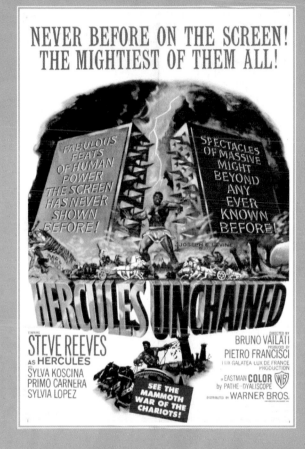

ABOVE: *Hercules Unchained.* One-sheet 1959. (U.S.A.)

MONSTER vs GOLIATH...ALL NEW...THE MIGHTIEST BATTLE OF THEM ALL!

DINO DE LAURENTIIS PRESENTS
GORDON SCOTT STARRING IN

GOLIATH AND THE VAMPIRES

IN COLORSCOPE

SEE: the revolt of the faceless humanoids!
SEE: the holocaust in the cave of fire!
SEE: the torture chamber of the blue men!
SEE: the lost island of the vampires!
SEE: the virgin-harem of the vampire god!

Also Starring
GIANNA MARIA CANALE · JACQUES SERNAS · GIACOMO GENTILOMO · AN AMERICAN INTERNATIONAL PICTUR

Directed by

COPYRIGHT © 1964 AMERICAN INTERNATIONAL PICTURES PRINTED IN U.S.A.

and the Sins of Babylon, we are treated to an image of the bound but aggressively muscular Mark Forest; however, to make the situation even clearer, we read above him, "See the thousand and one orgies of torture! The nights of pleasure . . . the days of terror!" In *Hercules and the Captive Women,* this sexual teasing is taken to its extreme as viewers are asked, "What sadistic secret did these women possess? Could she subdue this giant of a man with her sorcery?" In the half-sheet version of the poster, there is even less doubt about what this "sorcery" consists of, since a bound woman kneels literally between the widely planted legs of a Greco-Roman soldier; in his hand a phallic cup drips wine suggestively, while a bejeweled arrow-like brooch points directly to the woman's crotch. A representation of a monster-carrying Hercules appears off to the side, but he is definitely an auxiliary figure. It is easy to imagine adolescent boys digging deeply in their pockets for the requisite coins to buy a ticket to this carnival of sensuality[8].

As in most carnivals, the promises rarely matched the delivered goods, and *Hercules and the Captive Women* is no different. It is no more salacious than any other film of the time, but the poster designers knew how to tempt an audience into buying tickets. Like the films themselves, they quickly learned to use subtext, hint, and innuendo as effectively as the moviemakers.

North American and European males might well have wondered if they were being beguiled into a sensuous world of homoeroticism; after all, the main characters of these epics were handsome, muscular men whose usual costumes were designed to display their

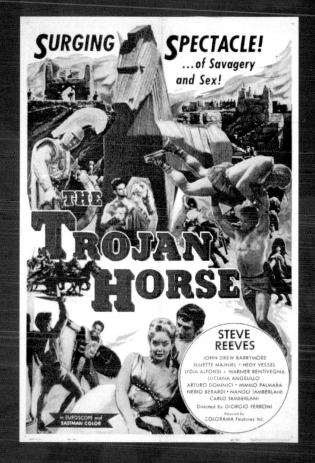

ABOVE: *The Trojan Horse.* One-sheet 1961. Typically cluttered design makes it difficult to understand this poster, but the "savagery and sex" are promised loudly and clearly. (U.S.A.) OPPOSITE: *Goliath and the Vampires.* Half-sheet 1961. American designers seemed to have better luck with half-sheets than any other form of advertising. This poster is one of the better examples of U.S. design.

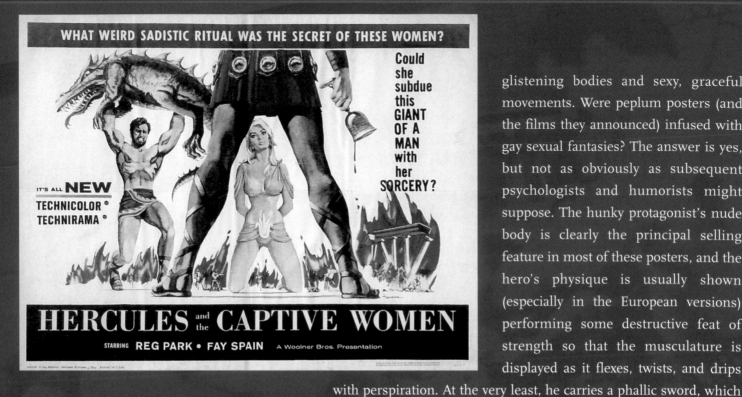

WHAT WEIRD SADISTIC RITUAL WAS THE SECRET OF THESE WOMEN?

Could she subdue this GIANT OF A MAN with her SORCERY?

IT'S ALL NEW
TECHNICOLOR®
TECHNIRAMA®

HERCULES and the CAPTIVE WOMEN

STARRING REG PARK • FAY SPAIN   A Woolner Bros. Presentation

ABOVE: *Hercules and the Captive Women.* Half-sheet 1961. Although there are no captive women in this movie, there are enough suggestive illustrations to make this one of the sexiest posters in peplum history. (U.S.A.) OPPOSITE: *Goliath and the Barbarians.* Record cover 1959. In US and British versions of this film, the original main title score by Carlo Innocenzi was replaced by a score by Les Baxter. The soundtrack recording was then released to help promote the film.

glistening bodies and sexy, graceful movements. Were peplum posters (and the films they announced) infused with gay sexual fantasies? The answer is yes, but not as obviously as subsequent psychologists and humorists might suppose. The hunky protagonist's nude body is clearly the principal selling feature in most of these posters, and the hero's physique is usually shown (especially in the European versions) performing some destructive feat of strength so that the musculature is displayed as it flexes, twists, and drips with perspiration. At the very least, he carries a phallic sword, which is either upright and ready for action or hanging down between bouts[9]. There is no denying the sexual appeals inherent in these representations, and since the obvious target audience for the films was masculine, the conclusion is clear that the stars' bodies are being displayed for reasons that almost certainly include sensual attraction. But this was far from the only reason.

On those rare occasions when it appears in films or magazines, the naked male body makes most heterosexual North American men very nervous, so society has devised several alibis for its display. One of these is when the musculature is objectified and displayed as in bodybuilding competitions, but another more common excuse is

ORIGINAL MOTION PICTURE SOUNDTRACK
Music Composed by Les Baxter

'I will kill 10,000 barbarians... and they will call me GOLIATH'!

JAMES H. NICHOLSON & SAMUEL Z. ARKOFF present

STEVE REEVES as

GOLIATH

when a man's nude muscles are engaged in some sort of destruction. Red-blooded American men can happily watch a shirtless Rambo shoot bad guys or enjoy the pratfalls of semi-naked professional wrestlers, but they immediately become nervous when a male strips for action intending to pursue goals other than mindless violence.

Although European males are generally less bothered by male nudity, they too feel better when there is a little mayhem involved. Thus, the sword-and-sandal posters show the semi-nude hero slashing, throwing, wrestling, or lifting real or improvised weapons. In this way, the poster artists neatly avoid the problem of alienating

TOP LEFT: *Hercules against Rome.* Large one-sheet. The film's star is Alan Steel, but it is Gordon Scott's portrait that is displayed. (ITALY) **LEFT:** *Goliath and the Rebel Slave.* Large one-sheet.
ABOVE: *Hercules and the Tyrants of Babylon.* Lobby card 1965. (U.S.A.)

their hetero clientele while simultaneously attracting the homo fans. The sexual innuendos were there to lure knowing customers, and the promise of physical action attracted younger audiences who were eager at the same time to explore the mysteries of sex. Therefore, the peplum offered something for everyone young, old, gay, straight— everyone, that is, except women.

Muscular males are clearly at the center of the visual "sales pitch," but what about the females in peplum posters? How are they portrayed? The answer is one that would set the teeth of most feminists on edge: women are relegated to a couple of stereotyped roles, neither of which gives females much credit. Those looking for images of spunky, in-your-face, independent women will be hard pressed to find them in either gladiator films or the movie posters that advertised them. Jon Solomon in *The Ancient World in the Cinema* best describes the role of women in this genre: "The chesty hero has a charmingly innocent and chesty girlfriend . . . and she is adept at virtuously bathing the hero's wounds (generally only flesh wounds on the shoulder) and keeping her plunging-necked tunic from plunging too far.[10]" She is always getting into scrapes from which only her heroic boyfriend can rescue her.

The heroine is almost always blond, unlike the other stereotyped female who inhabits Peplumland, the dark-haired, evil bitch queen. She is usually spurned by the muscular hero early in the film, and spends the rest of the movie trying to wreak her cruel revenge. Of the two, the evil brunette is invariably more interesting than her insipid light-haired sister.[11]

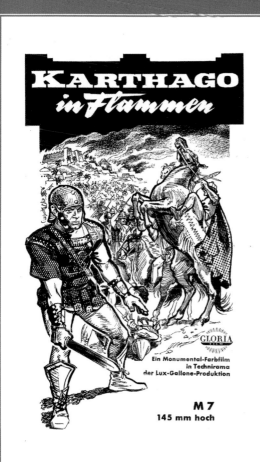

ABOVE: *Carthage in Flames.* Newspaper ad. (GERMANY)

WANTON...TEMPTRESS
...FLAME-HAIRED FIREBRAND...
SHE PUT THE TORCH
TO AN EMPIRE OF SIN!

No man could tame her...
No chains could hold her...
This wild beauty who took
by storm what she could
not take by love!

THE REVOLT OF THE SLAVES
in COLOR

starring
RHONDA   LANG   DARIO   with GINO
FLEMING · JEFFRIES · MORENO · CERVI

RAFAEL   WANDISA   ETTORE
RIVELLES · GUIDA · MANNI   Screenplay by
                                  DUCCIO TESSARI and
                                  STEFANO STRUCCHI

Dialogue by   Directed by   Produced by
DANIEL MAINWARING · NUNZIO MALASOMMA · PAOLO MOFFA
Print by TECHNICOLOR · Released thru UNITED UA ARTISTS   Photographed in
                                                          EASTMANCOLOR
                                                          and TOTALSCOPE

THEATRE

2 Cols. x 126 Lines—252 Lines (18 Col. Inches)   Mat 205

LEFT: The *Revolt of the Slaves*. Newspaper ad 1961. (U.S.A.)

Women are almost always relegated to inferior places in North American posters. The "good" girl is most often portrayed in a prone position (usually cringing in terror) at the hero's feet, chastely supporting herself on the thigh of Hercules, clinging protectively to the hero or awaiting rescue (usually tied to a stake) with an anguished expression on her face. The "bad" girl is usually flicking a whip, clinging (this time seductively) to the upright hero, or simply glaring in icy, malevolent hatred. In this hyper-masculine fantasy world, it is up to the man to resist the impure advances of the one and rescue the other from various fates worse than death.

Women scarcely fare better in European posters. Images of women (when they appear at all) are shown as either disembodied heads floating extraneously in the corners or bound and gagged, cringing piteously in the background, anxiously awaiting deliverance. Females were clearly not the empowered sisterhood that they are now—these are girls who are in serious need of rescuing by the nearest muscular stud. There is no new ground cultivated in these films when it comes to the relations between the sexes, but perhaps this was an important but unspoken reason for their meteoric popularity.

For whatever reasons, the muscle movie craze swept the world with astounding speed and thoroughness. In 1957, the year *Hercules* was produced, only ten costume dramas were made in Italy. By 1960, thirty-seven of these sword-and-sandal epics had been made, and in the next four years a great many more were produced in Italy or by Italian companies in conjunction with French, Spanish, German, American, or Yugoslavian companies. The peplum phenomenon quickly mushroomed into a major form of crowd-pleasing entertainment. These *filone*, or formula films, were Italy's unsung contribution to world cinema, and Italian producers learned how to churn out an amazing number of films using recycled sets, stock footage, and supporting players. Eventually, the total number of gladiator films reached nearly 200—ten percent of the total output of Italy's film industry between 1958 and 1964.[12]

As popular as these films were with the general public, they did not earn much critical acclaim. Their repetitive plots, hokey, dubbed dialogue, and often cheesy sets condemned them to critical Hades. The *New York Times* reviews are typical of the notices that these films received from the dagger-sharp pens of most critics. *The Mighty Crusaders* (1961), for instance, is called "just another hunk of gaudy Gorgonzola from the Italian 'poverty row.'" *Attila* (1958) is denounced as a "pointless fudge of violence and piety," and even *Hercules* is ridiculed as "one of the funniest pictures to reach U.S. screens in years—although the humor is not deliberate."[13] Devising funny, dismissive one-liners may have been as easy as shooting fish in an amphora, but it does not explain the incredible popularity of the films. For that we must look deeper.

Like all works of art, the gladiator movies of the 1960s were reflections of their time, and an examination of why the phenomenon

TOP RIGHT: *The Revolt of the Slaves*. Small one-sheet. Rhonda Fleming starred in this remake of *Fabiola* with her husband, Lang Jeffries. (FRANCE) RIGHT: *Sword of the Conqueror*. One-sheet 1961. Jack Palance tried his hand at the peplum genre in this story of the Lombards vs. the Gepids. (U.S.A.)

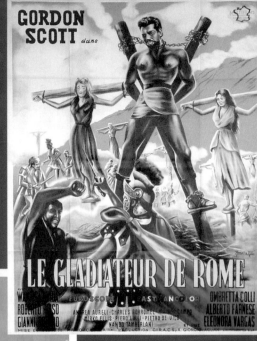

ABOVE: *The Gladiator of Rome.*
Large one-sheet. Although the artwork is crude, the design of this
poster conveys a haunting quality
that is largely absent from others.
(FRANCE) LEFT: *Maciste. The
Strongest Man in the World.* Large
one-sheet. (ITALY)

became popular when it did can reveal much about that era. As we have already noted, the first movie in the genre was *Hercules,* which appeared in 1959 in North America.[14] Why did this film make enough of an impact to propel the others that came after it to popularity and success?

Part of the reason for the triumph of *Hercules* can be traced to the era when they were produced. Italy, the birthplace of the peplum film, was emerging from its postwar devastation, and it was looking for a bit of diversion. What better way to forget the problems of the mid-twentieth century world than by harkening back to a time when Italy and other Mediterranean civilizations held sway over the entire world.

Ironically, the late 1950s and early 1960s was also the time when Italian neo-realism was creating a big stir in art houses and highbrow cinemas in both Europe and America. Many Italians were aware of this movement but did not want to be reminded of their distress and poverty. Like thousands of others across Europe caught in the vice of misery, many (perhaps most) Italians preferred to escape into the Technicolor, wide-screened confections then being produced at Cinecittà, the famous studio just outside Rome. Audiences wanted to escape as far from reality as possible, and these films came along at just the right time to provide that diversion.

In addition, there was added interest in the country's classical past because the 1960 Olympic Games were to be held in Rome, and the nation was consumed in nationalistic fervor not seen since the days of Mussolini. Muscular physiques and athletic competition were on the minds of many in the country, and it became fashionable to celebrate the muscular athletic body just as it had been in the bad old days under Il Duce.

For fans of these films around the world, there were other, more profound reasons for the success enjoyed by peplum movies. These productions represented machismo's last and finest moment; after the advent of the women's liberation movement, men could no longer glory in their own masculinity so thoroughly—especially at the expense of women. The protagonists of peplum movies used brute force to fight against tyranny in ways that contemporary men could not. Here were heroes who righted wrongs, saved damsels, disdained a sedentary life, and used righteous indignation and justly applied violence to solve problems. The audience no doubt longed for a gladius to cut through the Gordian knot of bureaucracy or to knock sense into those who opposed them. Such behavior might not have been possible in real life, but the men in the audience could identify

ABOVE: *The Queen of the Amazons*, locandina. Lighting, action scenes and romance were all typical ingredients of the peplum, and all are present in this work. (ITALY)

ABOVE: *The Witch's Curse.* One-sheet 1961. Bold, 1960s design makes this poster one of the best of the genre. (U.S.A.)

with Hercules and wish for similar easy solutions in the modern world. Soon, producers of sword-and-sandal movies attempted to inject variety into the genre, but not so much as to tamper with the time-honored premise.

As the peplum genre expanded, so did the acceptable locations of the plots. It became acceptable to see the mythical heroes of a Greco-Roman past washed up on the shores of the Inca empire (*Hercules vs. the Sons of the Sun*), in seventeenth-century Scotland (*The Witch's Curse*), nineteenth-century Russia (*Maciste and the Treasure of the Czars*) or even the American West (*Lost Treasure of the Aztecs*). By the mid-1960s, producers were trying every possible combination in order to keep the genre fresh and theater seats full.

The peplum can take place almost anywhere, but one ingredient of the formula is immutable: the film must have a shirtless, muscular hero. For the first time in film history, male rather than female beauty is consistently touted as a selling point. Films of the 1950s featured many gorgeous female bombshells and bosomy sex goddesses, from Mamie Van Doren to Marilyn Monroe, but good-looking men were usually relegated to a minor place in the bedroom farces of previous eras. Certainly, there had been anomalies such as Valentino, Rock Hudson, or William Holden whose bodies had been exploited as things of beauty and sexual attraction, but the peplums kicked that concept up several notches.[15] Here was a whole series of movies that took as one of its principal themes the glorification of studly muscles and ruggedly handsome faces.

One of the indisputable ways that a peplum poster can be distinguished from any other genre is the presence of a shirtless bodybuilder. The hero's glistening muscles, straining sinews, and scantily clad physique all proclaim that here is a peplum film. Bodybuilding in the 1960s was still considered the recreation of a few cranks or narcissists of unreliable sexuality, but all that would change, and part of that change can be laid at the sandaled feet of the peplum hero. It became okay, even cool, to go to the gym and try to look like Steve Reeves or Gordon Scott. Everyone in Europe knew where to find people like that: America. Consequently, almost every sword-and-sandal poster prominently featured the name of some Anglo-Saxon star rather than a homegrown hunk. Ed Fury, Mark Forest, Rock Stevens, Gordon Scott, and Samson Burke were all summoned to Cinecittà and made a modest fortune heading up a polyglot cast.[16] When there were not enough Anglo-American bodybuilders to be found for the huge demand, local athletes were discovered and given new names. Thus, Frenchman Georges Marchal became anglicized to George Marshall, Giuliano Gemma often appeared under the name of Montgomery Wood, Kirk Morris had been born Adriano Bellini, and the blond Italian hunk Sergio Ciani was known to peplum fans as Alan Steel. Clearly, the producers of these films were keenly aware of what was in a name.[17]

By the mid to late 1960s, it mattered little whether or not the names were easy for Americans to pronounce. Gladiator films had run their course, and moviegoers were ready for something else.

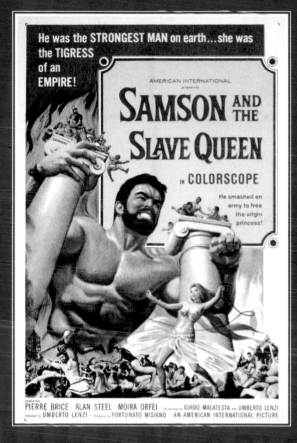

ABOVE: *Samson and the Slave Queen*. One-sheet 1963. (U.S.A.)

STEVE REEVES
LA GUERRA DI T

in
ROIA

Fortunately, the filone producers at Cinecittà were ready to change gears, and Italian studios began churning out spaghetti westerns, Mafia movies, and James Bond knockoffs. The same production machines that had turned out peplum movies supplied the new wave of films; thus the same actors who had been semi-naked in earlier posters now showed up in films and on posters wearing cowboy gear or silk suits and skinny ties. Ironically, the plots were virtually the same as the old peplums: a strong, ruggedly handsome stranger arrives on the scene and remedies injustice by restoring the good guys to their rightful places and destroying the bad guys. The ancient gladius had merely been replaced by a pistol—a different but no less phallic weapon.

Every few years, we are treated to new versions of the old peplum myths. *Conan the Barbarian*, *Hercules*, and *Gladiator* are all just recent reincarnations and reinterpretations of the immortal genre that has been with us since the beginnings of cinema. The sons of Hercules will continue to reappear on our televisions and movie screens, because we enjoy seeing good triumph over evil and we like celebrating physical beauty and fitness. Both qualities are given visible form in these muscle movie posters from around the world.

LEFT: *The Trojan War*, fotobusta. (ITALY)

efore Steve Reeves starred in *Hercules*, other films that were set in ancient times and which emphasized beefy heroes were popular all over the world. The Italians were the first to introduce muscular stars when in 1913 they began to make extravagant multi-reel films based on the splendors of ancient Rome. Silent versions of *Quo Vadis* and *Spartacus* were both made in that year. The peplum genre took off in a blaze of glory in 1914 with the release of *Cabiria*, which featured a well-built shirtless character named Maciste. A few films set in ancient times were made after that, but in the late 1940s and 1950s, huge Biblical epics came back in style with such films as *Samson and Delilah* (1949), *Quo Vadis* (1951), and *The Robe* (1953). The groundwork was thus laid for the peplum renaissance that began in 1959.

LEFT: *Demetrius and the Gladiators*, Finnish 1954. OPPOSITE: Hand-tinted theater slide from *The Last Days of Pompeii*, USA 1935.

THE LAST DAYS OF POMPEII

MERIAN C. COOPER'S
GIGANTIC SPECTACLE DRAMA

VESUVIUS
IS RAGING!
Run for your
lives!

One of the most
astounding big
scenes ever
screened is the
climax of a love
story 2,000
years old, that
will live to the
end of time!

PRESTON FOSTER
ALAN HALE
BASIL RATHBONE
JOHN WOOD
LOUIS CALHERN
DAVID HOLT
DOROTHY WILSON
WYRLEY BIRCH

DIRECTED BY
ERNEST B. SCHOEDSACK
RKO RADIO PICTURE

THE MIGHTIEST...
MOST MAGNIFICENT SCREEN
SPECTACLE EVER MADE!...

Fabulous
"Fabiola"

Goddess Of Love
In A City Of Sin!

SEE Splendid pageantry, lusty grandeur—in wicked, sinful, pagan Rome.

SEE A cast of 50,000... hordes of victims led to their doom in the Colosseum ... in history's most agonizing moments of terror!

SEE Giant gladiators fight to the death... in the screen's most savage scenes of mortal combat!

SEE The greatest love story ever filmed... emotion so fiery it defies all tortures... and certain death!

Jules Levey presents "FABIOLA" starring
MICHELE MORGAN · HENRI VIDAL · MICHEL SIMON
Screenplay & Directed by Alessandro Blasetti
English Language Adaptation by Marc Connelly & Fred Pressburger
Based on the novel "Fabiola" by Nicholas Wiseman
RELEASED THRU UNITED ARTISTS

BOTTOM LEFT: Pagano plays a coal stoker in *Maciste's Journey*, French, 1926.
BOTTOM RIGHT: *Fabiola*. Stylish French poster for this story of Christian persecution in ancient Rome, 1947. TOP LEFT: *Fabiola*. American half-sheet. It is reported that scenes of nude females sacrificed to the lions and crucified were removed from the US version.

Le Voyage de Maciste

ATELIERS SUPER VERSAILLES, PARIS 8me Cité Tréhisé

FRANCO · LONDON · FILM · EXPORT présente
Une Production SALVO D'ANGELO
Réalisée par UNIVERSALIA Paris, Rome

MICHÈLE MORGAN · MICHEL SIMON · LOUIS SALOU · HENRI VIDAL
FABIOLA
Inspiré du célèbre roman de WISEMAN
Mise en scène d'ALEXANDRE BLASETTI
GINO CERVI · ELISA CEGANI · MASSIMO GIROTTI

LEFT: *Samson and Delilah.* Canadian one-sheet 1949.

ABOVE: *O.K. Nero!* American two-sheet 1954. Comedy based on time travel and absurd anachronisms. The tagline "Quo Laughter!" shows that the film was probably meant to parody *Quo Vadis.*

ABOVE: *The Spartan Gladiators.* One-sheet 1965.

he decade of the 1950s was politically conservative in the United States, and Americans wanted to see their traditional values reflected and glorified in the movies. Because of this, cast-of-thousands Biblical films became very popular. Audi-ences were primed for ancient epics by the time Steve Reeves ap-peared in *Hercules,* and moviegoers discovered that they could enjoy action and half-naked protagonists without the preachy morality. Soon, Americans were just as seduced by peplum films as Europeans, and the gladiatorial floodgates had been opened.

Because these films were made in Italy where dubbing voices was the norm, they often were renamed before coming to North America. Thus, a character could be called "Maciste" in a foreign version of a film and "Samson" or "Hercules" in the American version. Audiences did not really care that the actors' lips were not in synch when the names were spoken. This also meant that titles could be changed at will, and if the movie was re-released later, the same film could end up with many different names. Despite these drawbacks, chronologies of American releases are much better documented so I have included dates in this section.

SEE THE **THOUSAND** AND **ONE** ORGIES OF **TORTURE!**

The Nights of Pleasure...
The Days of Terror!

AMERICAN INTERNATIONAL presents
IN COLOR AND TECHNISCOPE

GOLIATH AND THE SINS OF BABYLON

STARRING **MARK FOREST**

WITH JOSE GRECI and GULIANO GEMMA · Directed by MICHELE LUPO · Produced by ELIO SCARDAMAGLIA · Story and Screenplay by ROBERTO GIANVITI and FRANCESCO SCARDAMAGLIA

THE MONSTER THAT ROCKED A LOST CIVILIZATION!

Stalking out of a time of unbridled passion
and terror it comes...the half-man,
half-beast that made a civilization
bow down before it—and feed
its gargantuan lusts!

THE MINOTAUR

THE WILD BEAST OF CRETE

STARRING **BOB** MATHIAS · ROSANNA SCHIAFFINO · ALBERTO LUPO · RICK BATTAGLIA

Screenplay by S. CONTINENZA · G.P. CALLEGARI · DANIEL MAINWARING · Directed by SILVIO AMADIO · Produced by AGLIANI-MORDINI-ILLIRIA FILM
TECHNICOLOR · TOTALSCOPE · RELEASED THRU UNITED UA ARTISTS

ABOVE: *Goliath and the Sins of Babylon.* One-sheet 1963. The poster is a masterpiece of sado-masochistic titillation. **RIGHT:** *The Minotaur, the Wild Beast of Crete.*
One-sheet 1961. Olympic champion Bob Mathias stars in this epic.

THE SCREEN EXPLODES WITH WONDROUS **COLORSCOPE** SPECTACLE!!

SEE! **XNOBIA** SLAVE QUEEN OF THE BARBARIANS
SEE! **BATHSHEBA** VIRGIN QUEEN OF THE ORIENT
SEE! 10,000 HORSEMEN CHARGE THE VALLEY OF BLOOD
SEE! THE AMAZING FIRE THROWING CATAPULTS OF WAR
SEE! THE BARBARIAN TORTURE CATACOMBS OF HORROR
SEE! THE DESTRUCTION OF A MIGHTY PAGAN EMPIRE

THE ORGY OF THE PAGAN SLAVES

SACRIFICE OF THE VIRGIN IN THE TEMPLE OF RA

JAMES H. NICHOLSON and SAMUEL Z. ARKOFF present

SIGN OF THE GLADIATOR

STARRING ANITA EKBERG · LORELLA DE LUCA · GEORGE MARSHAL · JACQUE SERNAS   A GLOMER FILM PRODUCTION · AN AMERICAN INTERNATIONAL PICTURE

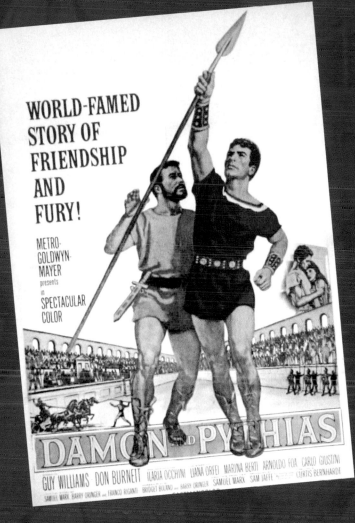

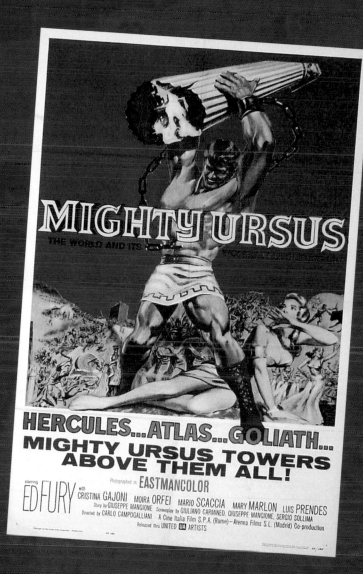

ABOVE: *Damon and Pythias.* One-shoot 1962. RIGHT: *The Mighty Ursus.* One-sheet 1960. A horizontal heroine, a pillar-wielding muscleman and bold colors all make a quintessential American sword-and-sandal poster. OPPOSITE: *Sign of the Gladiator.* Half-sheet 1959. The title to this is misleading; there are no gladiators in the film.

ABOVE: *Seven Slaves against the World*. Half-sheet 1964.

TOP RIGHT: *The Saracens*. One-sheet 1963. RIGHT: *Hercules against the Moon Men*. Half-sheet 1964. A hero in peril, three monsters, cheesecake, Cosmicolor and Lunarscope all did their bit to lure customers into the theater. OPPOSITE: *Goliath and the Dragon*. Half-sheet 1960. The film received scathing reviews (one critic said that the dragon looked like a fugitive from a kiddie puppet show), but the poster is interesting and well done.

AMAZING! FANTASTIC! OVERWHELMING!
The mightiest adventure of them all!

JAMES H. NICHOLSON AND SAMUEL Z. ARKOFF
present

GOLIATH AND THE DRAGON IN COLORSCOPE

Starring MARK FOREST · BRODERICK CRAWFORD · ELEONORA RUFFO
AND A CAST OF THOUSANDS · AN AMERICAN INTERNATIONAL PICTURE

MAN on earth...she was the TIGRESS of an EMPIRE!

He smashed an army to free the virgin princess!

AMERICAN INTERNATIONAL presents

SAMSON AND THE SLAVE QUEEN

ABOVE: *Samson and the 7 Miracles of the World.* One-sheet 1961. RIGHT: *Son of Samson.* One-sheet 1961. OPPOSITE: *Samson and the Slave Queen,* Lobby card 1963.

A MONSTER STATUE ...A FABULOUS FORTRESS
TWENTY STORIES TALL   ASTRIDE THE HARBOR OF RHODES!

METRO-GOLDWYN-MAYER
Presents
RORY CALHOUN

THE COLOSSUS OF RHODES

IN BLAZING
COLOR

with LEA MASSARI and GEORGES MARCHAL
CONRADO SAN MARTIN · ANGEL ARANDA

Directed by   Executive Producer
SERGIO LEONE · MICHELE SCAGLIONE

in SupertotalScope   Produced by CINEPRODUZIONI ASSOCIATE Rome
and EASTMANCOLOR   PRODUSA Madrid · C.F.P.C. and C.T.I. Paris

ABOVE: *The Giant of Marathon.* Half-sheet 1959.

TOP RIGHT: *Goliath and the Barbarians.* Insert poster 1959.

RIGHT: *The Slave, The Son of Spartacus.* One-sheet 1962.

OPPOSITE: *The Colossus of Rhodes.* Half-sheet 1961. Sergio

Leone who later went on to popularize spaghetti westerns made

his directorial debut with this adventure film.

A THOUSAND TEMPTING BEAUTIES...THEY FOUGHT LIKE TEN THOUSAND UNCHAINED TIGERS!

AMAZONS OF ROME

LOUIS JOURDAN   SYLVIA SYMS   NICOLE COURCEL

RENAUD MARY JEAN CHEVRIER NICOLAS VOGEL ETTORE MANNI with LEO JOANNON LUIGI EMMANUELE and GAETAN LOFFREDO

Produced and Directed by A French-Italian Co-production of Regina S.A., CARLO BRAGAGLIA Criterion Films S.A. (Paris) and Cine Italia (Rome) EASTMANCOLOR Released thru UNITED UA ARTISTS

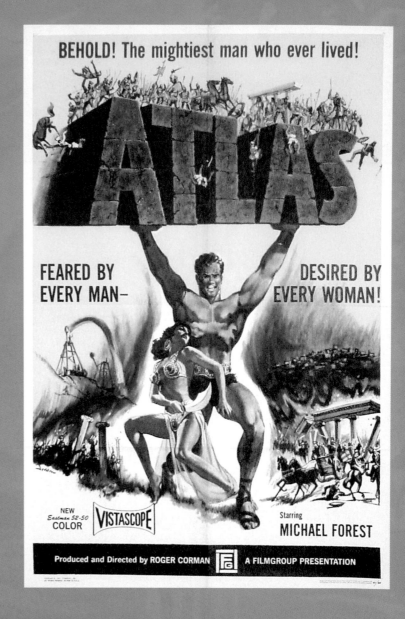

BEHOLD! The mightiest man who ever lived!

ATLAS

FEARED BY EVERY MAN—

DESIRED BY EVERY WOMAN!

NEW Eastman 52-50 COLOR   VISTASCOPE

Starring MICHAEL FOREST

Produced and Directed by ROGER CORMAN   A FILMGROUP PRESENTATION

ABOVE: *The Amazons of Rome*. One-sheet 1963. RIGHT: *Atlas*. One-sheet 1961. Roger Corman's attempt to cash in on the peplum craze. Atlas's power and potency are confirmed by the sword held at a suggestive height by the damsel who strokes the hero's thigh. This was strong stuff for the early 1960s!

OPPOSITE: *The Last Days of Pompeii*. Lobby card 1960.

TOP LEFT: *Revenge of the Gladiators.* One-sheet 1960. LEFT: *Conquest of Mycene.* One-sheet 1964.

Aside from misspelling "Mycenae," this sad poster was mainly cannibalized from illustrations taken

from other posters. ABOVE: *Gladiators Seven.* Four-sheet 1964.

ABOVE: *The Mighty Ursus.* Lobby card 1960.

LEFT: Second only to Steve Reeves in the number of gladiator movies that he made, Gordon Scott was one of the few peplum stars who was praised for his acting abilities.

TOP RIGHT: Before becoming a peplum star, Mark Forest achieved fame in the bodybuilding world under his given name, Lou Degni.

BOTTOM RIGHT: British championship bodybuilder Reg Park battles a boa in *Hercules and Captive Women.*

n addition to being advertising tools, French movie posters are nearly always beautiful works of art. Posters of any sort have long been viewed as works of art in France, whereas in America they are treated as litter after their purpose has been served. French posters are the largest general-use posters in the world. A large French one-sheet measures an impressive 45 1/2 x 61 1/2 inches, and the effect of such an expanse is usually very striking. Thanks to the vivid colors and the stone litho printing process, French cinema posters would be sought after by collectors at half the size.

ABOVE: *Hercules and the Queen of Lydia.* Small one-sheet. Steve Reeves' second film shows the muscular hero caught between the blond good girl and the redhead bad girl. Poor Herc never had a chance.

TOP LEFT: *Heroic Conquerors.* Small one-sheet.

MIDDLE: *The Son of Spartacus.* Large one-sheet.

RIGHT: *Helen, Queen of Troy.* Small one-sheet.

ABOVE: *Carthage in Flames*. Small one-sheet. MIDDLE: *The Three Stooges vs. Hercules*. Small one-sheet. Canadian bodybuilder Samson Burke's most famous role came in this popular pastiche of anachronistic gags. Burke later teamed up with the great Neapolitan comic Totò. RIGHT: *Taur, The King of Brute Strength*. Large one-sheet. Artist, Claude Belinsky. With all those spears aimed at Taur's crotch, no wonder he has a pained expression. OPPOSITE: *The Challenge of the Giants*. Large one-sheet.

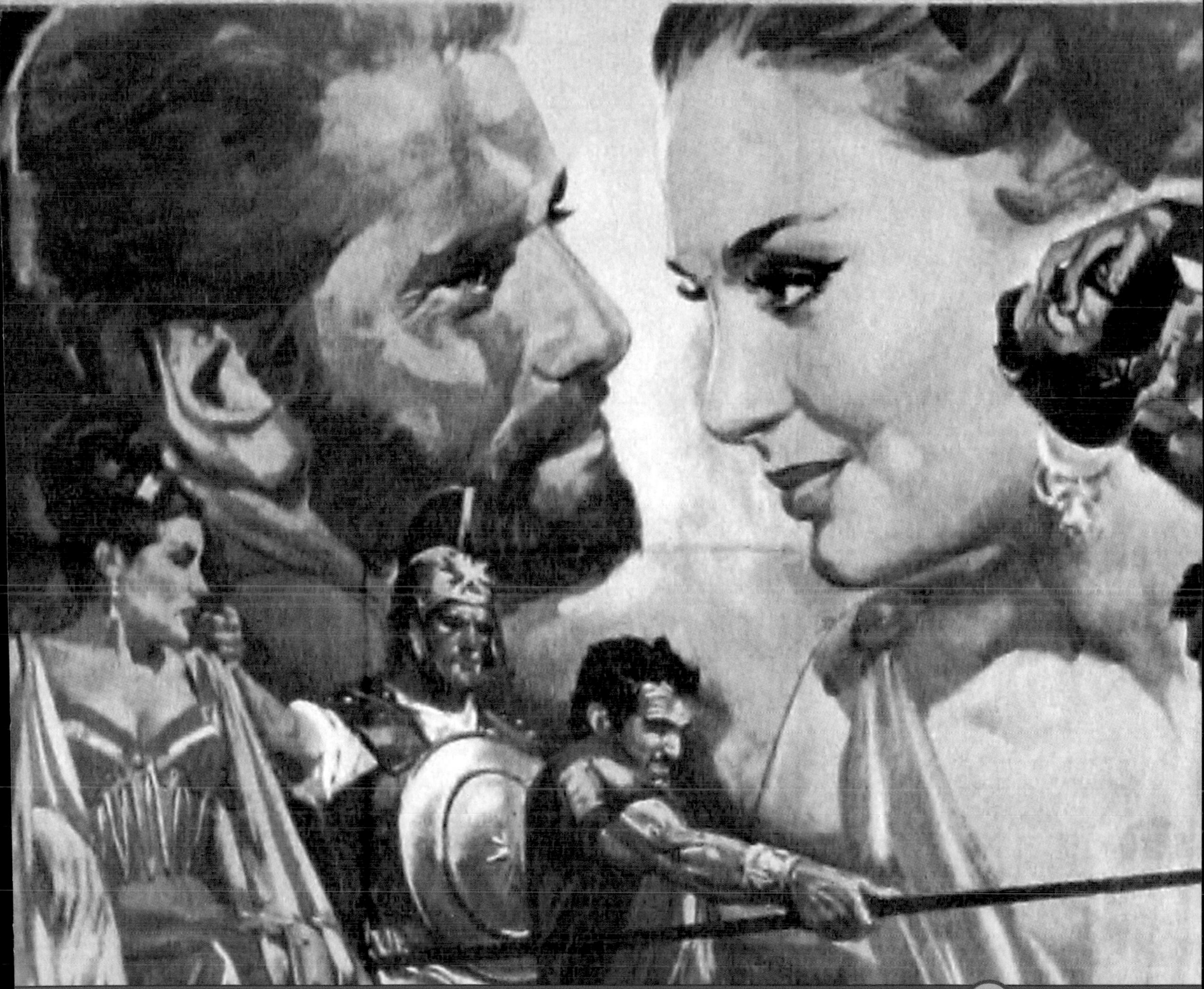

ABOVE: *The Hell of Genghis Khan.* Large one-sheet. Artist, Claude Belinsky. Apparently, the artist was hard pressed to find a single defining moment to convey the plot, so he created this bubbling bouillabaisse of excitement.

MIDDLE: *Maciste, the Strongest Man in the World.* Large one-sheet.

RIGHT: *Ulysses vs. Hercules.* Large one-sheet.

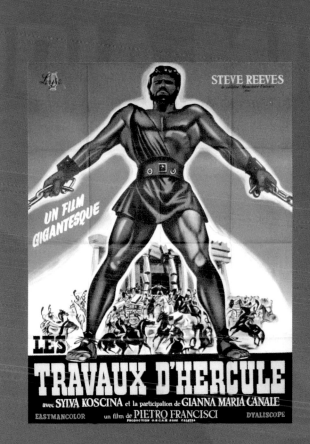

LEFT: *The Magnificent Gladiator.* Large one-sheet.

ABOVE: *The Labors of Hercules.* Large one-sheet.

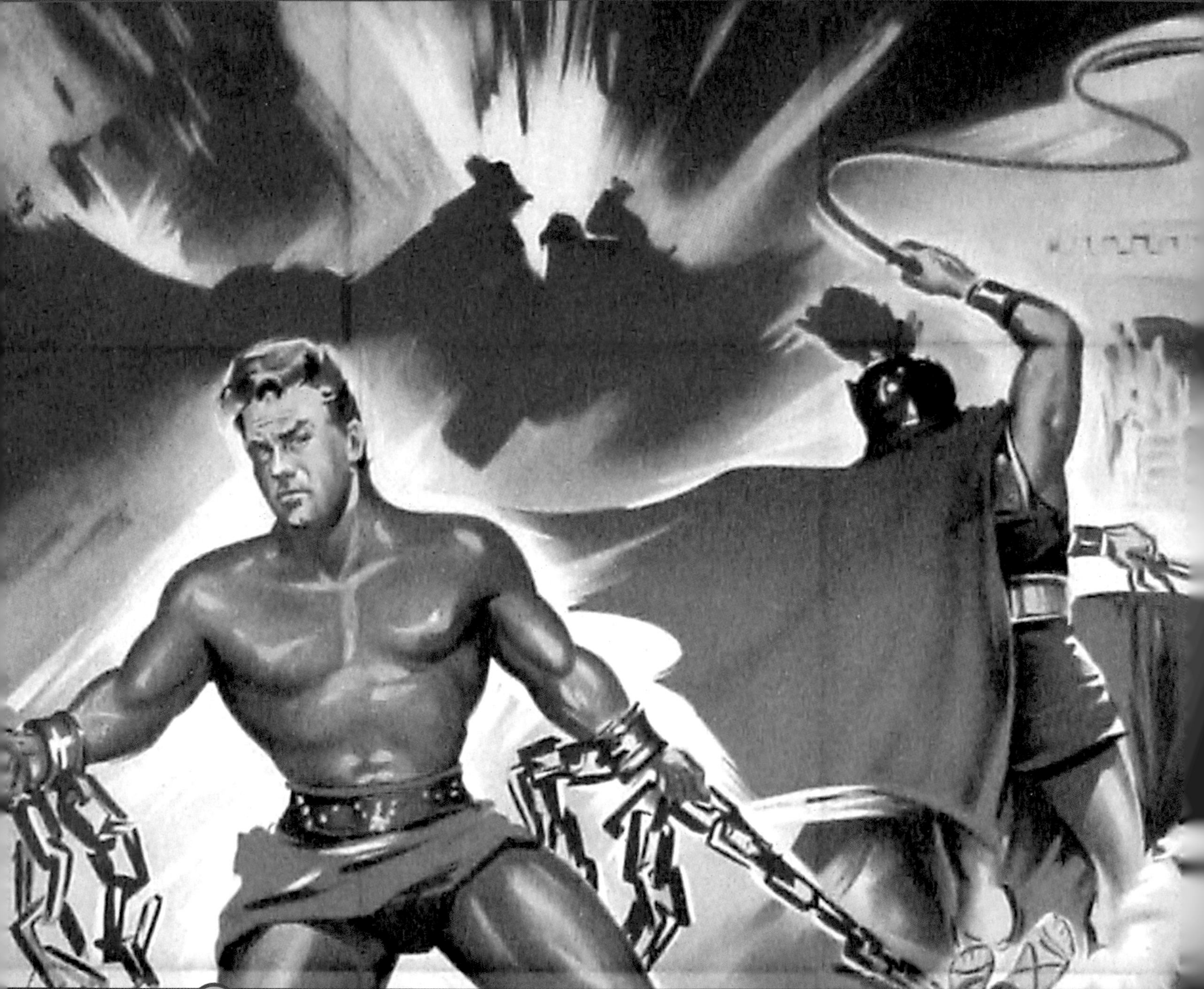

ABOVE: *Lightning over Babylon*. Large one-sheet. Artist, Claude Belinsky. One of the most bizarre designs for any peplum poster, this wonderful work is much better than the film it advertises. MIDDLE: *Pharaoh's Slave*. Large one-sheet. Artist, Claude Belinsky RIGHT: *Semiramis, Goddess of the Orient*. Large one sheet, Artist, Claude Belinsky OPPOSITE: *Ursus in the Land of Fire*. Large one-sheet. Artist, Claude Belinsky. The colors are bright, the action remarkable, but it's difficult to tell what's going on here. No matter, Ursus will save the girl.

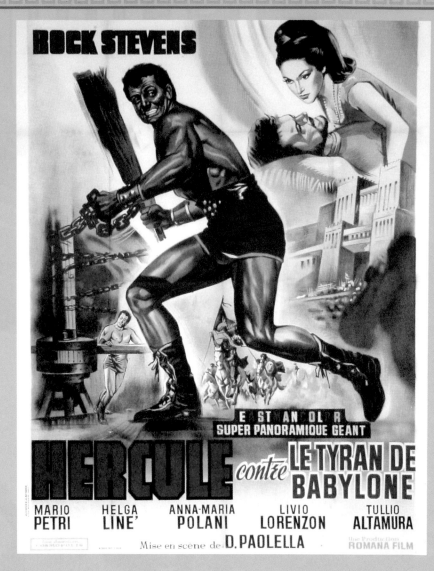

TOP LEFT: *Romulus and Remus.* Large one-sheet. The confrontation between these two brothers is superbly indicated by the split design and the lunging figures. Virna Lisi would do well to stay in the background. LEFT: *The Strongest Gladiators in the World.* Large one-sheet. Artist, Claude Belinsky. ABOVE: *Hercules against the Tyrant of Babylon.* Large one-sheet.

ABOVE: *The Treasure of the Czars.* Large one-sheet. Artist, Claude Belinsky. A rampaging, shirtless strongman in the court of the Czar? Why not? Anything is possible in Peplumland. MIDDLE: *The Wrath of Achilles.* Large one-sheet. Artist, Claude Belinsky. This is perhaps the artist's finest work. The angry hero glares out from his shining, black helmet and the body of Hector is dragged around the walls of Troy. The red of anger contrasts beautifully with the blue-black of cold fury. RIGHT: *Samson the Invincible.* Large one-sheet. Artist, Claude Belinsky.

LEFT: *Maciste in the Valley of the Lions.* Large one-sheet.

Artist, Claude Belinsky. ABOVE: *Maciste and the Girls of the*

Valley. Large one-sheet.

LEFT: *Perseus the Invincible*. Large one-sheet. Artist, Claude

Belinsky. ABOVE: *The Terror of the Kirghiz*. Large one-sheet.

Artist, Claude Belinsky. OVERLEAF: *Goliath against the Giants*.

Press book.

LES FILMS FERNAND RIVERS S. A.
présentent
UNE PRODUCTION CINEPRODUZIONI ASSOCIATE-Roma - PROCUSA-Madrid

BRAD HARRIS
GLORIA MILLAND

BARBARA CARROL

FERNANDO REY

JOSÉ RUBIO

LINA ROSALES

CARMEN DE LIRIO

Mise en scène
de
GUIDO MALATESTA

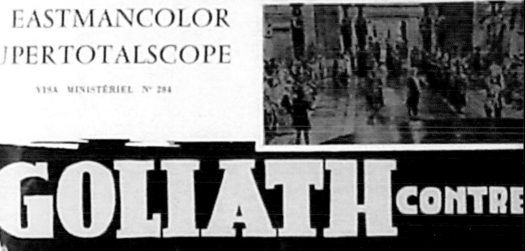

EASTMANCOLOR
SUPERTOTALSCOPE

VISA MINISTÉRIEL N° 284

GOLIATH CONTRE LES GEANTS

ABOVE: *The Invincible Maciste Brothers.* Large one-sheet. RIGHT: *The Daughter of the Tartars.*, Large one-sheet. OPPOSITE LEFT: *Goliath against the Giants.* Large one-sheet. Artist, Claude Belinsky. OPPOSITE RIGHT TOP: *Maciste against the Mongols.* Large one-sheet. Artist Claude Belinsky.

OPPOSITE RIGHT: *Alone against Rome.* Large one-sheet. Artist, Claude Belinsky.

ABOVE: *The Abduction of the Sabines.* Large one-sheet.

MIDDLE: *The Last Days of Herculaneum.* Large one-sheet.

RIGHT: *The Return of the Titans.* Large one-sheet.

OPPOSITE: *Julius Caesar vs. the Pirates.* Large one-sheet.

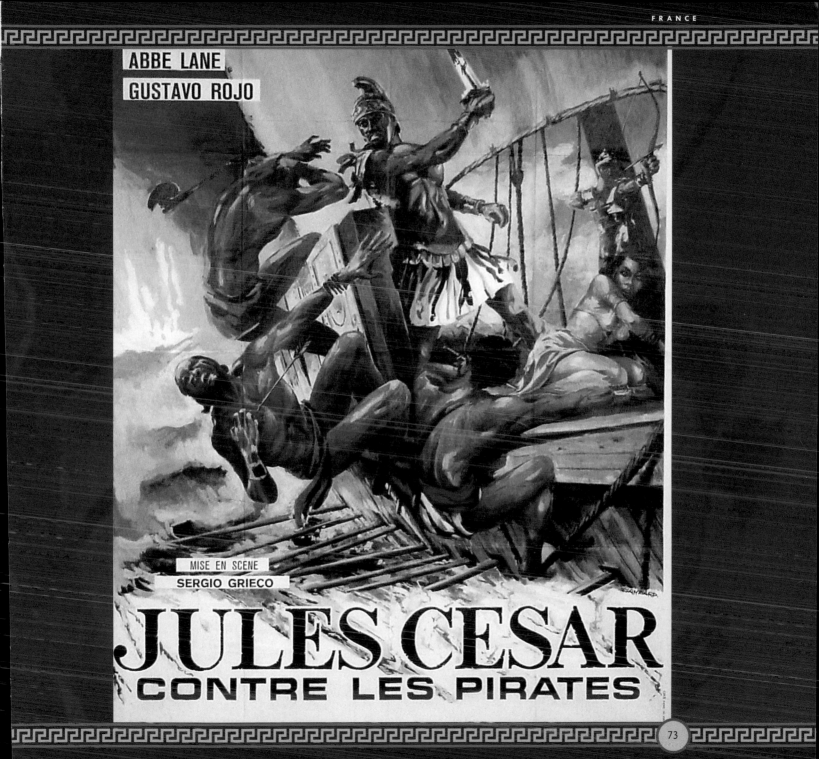

ABBE LANE
GUSTAVO ROJO

MISE EN SCENE
SERGIO GRIECO

JULES CESAR
CONTRE LES PIRATES

Je ne peux encore réaliser que tu sois vivant! Viens, buvons au Dieu Mars, puis tu me raconteras tes aventures!...

STAR CINE
VAILLANCE

LE
REBELLE
DE
ROME

LE PREMIER COUP DE FOUET S'ABAT SUR LA DOUCE PEAU DE SES ÉPAULES, LAISSANT UNE MARQUE SANGLANTE.

4° Année · N. 71
20 Juin 1964
1F 30
BELGIQUE: F.b. 17
CANADA: Cents 35
SUISSE: Fr. S. 1.20

RIGHT: The French often published comic book-like versions of a film in order to generate interest. These were variously called "Photozines" or "Film Color Novels" *The Rebel of Rome* is also known as *The Last Days of Herculaneum.*

ABOVE TOP: Photozine panel. "I still can't believe that you are alive! Come, let us drink to the god Mars, then you can tell me of your adventures." From the photozine for *The Conqueror of Corinth.* **ABOVE BOTTOM:** Photozine panel. "The first sting of the whip lashed the soft skin of her shoulders leaving a bloody mark." From the photozine for *The Virgins of Rome.*

ABOVE: A very chesty Dan Vadis appears ready for any eventuality. A smart-alecky British critic once wondered if Vadis might be the brother of Quo. MIDDLE: Richard Lloyd polishes off an evil leopard-man in *The Invincible Maciste Brothers*. RIGHT: Samson Burke was a Canadian athlete who starred in several peplum epics, most remarkably in *Hercules and the Three Stooges*.

MARK FOREST IN

MACISTE
contro i
MONGOLI

DON
KEN CLARKE · JOSE' GRECI
GRAZIA MARIA SPINA
RENATO ROSSINI
· REGIA DI DOMENICO PAOLELLA
EASTMANCOLOR - TOTALSCOPE

ANNO DI EDIZIONE MCMLXIII

Second only to France in the brilliance and beauty of poster design, these advertising sheets were clearly important to Italians. Since Italy is the home of the peplum, great care and expense were lavished on movie posters. Variety of design and color were not the only variations that Italian artists used, they also employed a great diversity of sizes in their movie advertising. These include the large one-sheet (39 x 55 inches), the small one-sheet (26 1/2 x 38) the locandina (27 1/2 x 13), the small fotobusta (18 1/2 x 26 1/2) and the large fotobusta (26 1/2 x 37).

LEFT: *Maciste vs. the Mongols,* locandina. The Italians were experts at the art of chiaroscuro, the contrast between the light and dark makes their posters dramatic. ABOVE: Steve Reeves relaxes between takes. Destroying temples can be fatiguing. OPPOSITE LEFT: *The Strongest Slaves in the World,* locandina. The heroism, beauty, and tragic isolation in the arena are all conveyed in this poster. OPPOSITE RIGHT: *Vulcan, Son of Jove,* locandina.

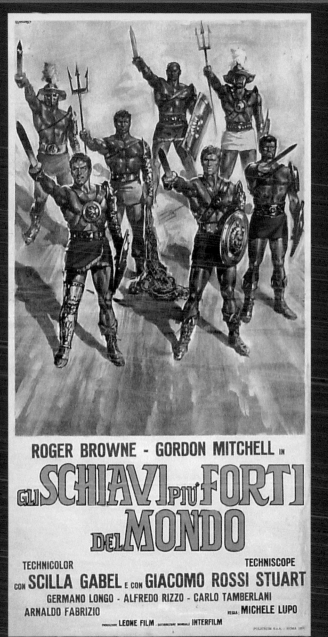

ROGER BROWNE - GORDON MITCHELL IN

GLI SCHIAVI PIÙ FORTI DEL MONDO

TECHNICOLOR   TECHNISCOPE

CON **SCILLA GABEL** E CON **GIACOMO ROSSI STUART**

GERMANO LONGO - ALFREDO RIZZO - CARLO TAMBERLANI

ARNALDO FABRIZIO   REGIA: MICHELE LUPO

PRODUZIONE **LEONE FILM** DISTRIBUZIONE MONDIALE **INTERFILM**

POLITECNI S.A.A. - ROMA 197

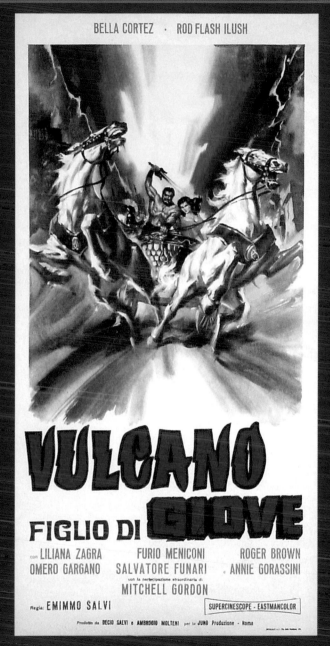

BELLA CORTEZ · ROD FLASH ILUSH

VULCANO FIGLIO DI GIOVE

CON LILIANA ZAGRA   FURIO MENICONI   ROGER BROWN
OMERO GARGANO   SALVATORE FUNARI · ANNIE GORASSINI

con la partecipazione straordinaria di
MITCHELL GORDON

Regia: EMIMMO SALVI   SUPERCINESCOPE - EASTMANCOLOR

Prodotto da DECIO SALVI e AMBROGIO MOLTENI per la JUNO Produzione - Roma

FORTUNATO MISIANO PRESENTA

UNA CO-PRODUZIONE ITALO-FRANCESE, ROMANA FILM, ROMA - S.F.F. ALFRED RODE, PARIGI

ALAN STEEL in

ERCOLE
CONTRO ROMA

DANIELE VARGAS WANDISA GUIDA (S.S.S.) LIVIO LORENZON ANDREA AURELI
TULLIO ALTAMURA - NELLO PAZZAFINI - CARLO TAMBERLANI
SIMONETTA SIMEONI - RENATO NAVARRINI - ANNA ARENA
ALBERTO CEVENINI - DINA DE SANTIS
E CON MIMMO PALMARA

REGIA DI PIERO PIEROTTI   EASTMANCOLOR - TOTALSCOPE

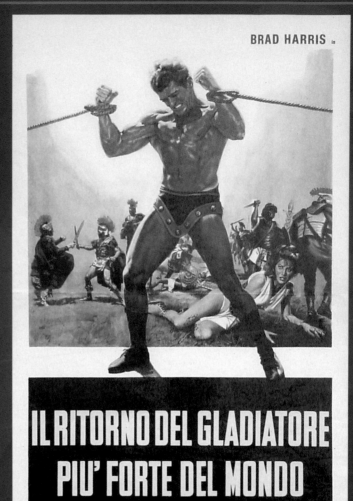

BRAD HARRIS in

IL RITORNO DEL GLADIATORE
PIU' FORTE DEL MONDO

CON

JOHN BARRACUDA   RAF BALDASSARRE   MICHEL LEMOINE

MARIA PIA CONTE   MARGARET ROSE KEIL   ADLER GRAY   PAOLO ROSANI   e   ALBERT FARLEY

Regia di AL ALBERT

Una produzione LEA FILM EASTMANCOLOR COLORSCOPE dalla S.P.E.S. Distribuzione INTERFILM

RIGHT: *Hercules vs. the Tyrants of Babylon,* locandina. One of the most dramatic designs of any poster, this one literally draws the viewer in to the world of ancient heroes.

OPPOSITE LEFT: *Hercules vs. Rome,* locandina.

OPPOSITE RIGHT: *The Return of the Strongest Gladiator in the World,* locandina. The artist explores the beauty and tension of the actor's muscled body. It is both exciting and erotic.

ABOVE: *Maciste in the Hell of Genghis Khan.* Large one-sheet. Drawing on the ancient sculpture of Laocoön, the poster artist pits Mark Forest against a vicious reptile. The Freudian implications are unmistakable to modern eyes, however.
MIDDLE: *Maciste in the Hell of Genghis Khan.* Fotobusta. RIGHT: *Maciste, the Avenger of the Mayas.* Large one-sheet. OPPOSITE LEFT: *Ulysses vs. Hercules,* locandina. OPPOSITE RIGHT: *The Gladiator of Rome,* locandina. The gladiator's net seems to be cast directly at the spectator, thus providing another beautiful example of the Italian genius for involving the viewer in the action.

BELOW: *The Battle of Marathon.* Fotobusta.

RIGHT: *The Revenge of Hercules.* Fotobusta.

BOTTOM RIGHT: Mark Forest prepares to whip

out his gladius.

DAN VADIS   KEN CLARK
SPELA ROZIN   JON SIMONS
CAROLL BRAWN

HUGO ARDEN · SAND BEANTY
RED ROSS · KIRK BERT
E CON
JEANETTE BARTON

ERCOLE L'INVINCIBILE

TECHNISCOPE · TECHNICOLOR

LA VENDETTA DI ERCOLE

MARK FOREST   BRODERICK CRAWFORD
REGIA VITTORIO COTTAFAVI   EASTMANCOLOR   PROD. PIAZZI-FUCHS

LEFT: *Hercules the Invincible*. Small one-sheet. One of the most famous poses in all peplum films: the hero resists the pull of two chains. No better pose for displaying the physique in all its straining splendor. ABOVE: *The Revenge of Hercules*. Large one-sheet. Chains, straining muscles and an ethereal female face make for powerful images. As in most Italian posters, it is the man's body that is the center of attention.

ABOVE: *Zorro vs. Maciste.* Large one-sheet. Two protagonists from different eras are brought together in this improbable mix of heroes. The masked man's black costume and pointing sword fit the genre neatly, however.

MIDDLE: *The Ten Gladiators.* Large one-sheet. RIGHT: *The Last Days of Pompeii.* Large one-sheet. This is a curiously unsophisticated example of Italian poster art. Perhaps it was influenced by American design.

ABOVE: *Samson.* Large one-sheet.

MIDDLE: *Ursus in the Valley of the Lions*

Large one-sheet. RIGHT: *The Colossus of*

Rome. Large one-sheet.

EASTMANCOLOR

LEFT: *Maciste vs. the Headhunters.* Large one-sheet. Maciste's anger is mirrored by the exploding volcano in the background. BELOW: *Maciste in the Land of the Cyclops.* Large one-sheet. OPPOSITE: *The Legend of Aeneas.* Two-sheet. This large work displays chiaroscuro to excellent effect: the dark figure in the foreground with his menacing, spiky helmet is clearly a bad guy about to be finished off by Aeneas.

ABOVE: *Samson vs. the Pirates.* Large one-sheet.

MIDDLE: *The Invincible Maciste Brothers.* Large one-sheet. RIGHT: *A Sword for the Empire.* Large one-sheet.

URSUS GLADIATORE RIBELLE

DAN VADIS · JOSÉ GRECI · GIANNI SANTUCCIO · GLORIA MILLAND
EASTMANCOLOR · TECHNISCOPE
REGIA DI DOMENICO PAOLELLA

MACISTE CONTRO LO SCEICCO

ED FURY · ERNO CRISA · GISELLA ARDEN
REGIA DOMENICO PAOLELLA   CINEMASCOPE · EASTMANCOLOR

PROD. C.I.G.F.

BRAD HARRIS

GOLIATH CONTRO I GIGANTI

BARBARA CARROL · FERNANDO REY · JOSE' RUBIO · LINA ROSALES
CARMEN DE LIRIO
REGIA GUIDO MALATESTA
EASTMANCOLOR · CINEMASCOPE

ABOVE: *Ursus, Rebel Gladiator.* Large one-sheet.
This startling image of a man being drowned is
both beautiful and brutal. MIDDLE: *Maciste vs. the
Sheik.* Large one-sheet. RIGHT: *Goliath
vs. the Giants.* Large one-sheet.

ABOVE: *Maciste vs. the Vampire.* Large one-sheet. Gorgeously moody poster, with the eerie blues of the background contrasted with the warm flesh tones of the two men in the foreground. ABOVE RIGHT: *Maciste, Gladiator of Sparta.*

Large one-sheet. RIGHT: Gordon Scott attempts to wriggle out of his chains.

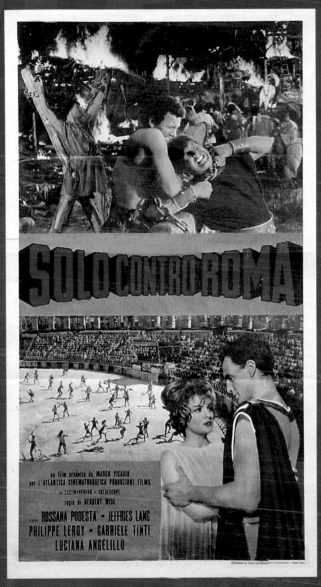

ABOVE: *Alone against Rome*, locandina. TOP RIGHT: *The Conqueror of Atlantis*. Fotobusta. RIGHT: *The Conqueror of Atlantis*. Fotobusta.

TOP LEFT: *Totò vs. Maciste.* Fotobusta. The great Neapolitan comic Totò is here teamed with Samson Burke in this amusing parody of the peplum genre. BOTTOM LEFT: *Totò vs. Maciste.* Fotobusta. ABOVE: *The Loves of Hercules.* Large fotobusta.

LEFT: *The Wrath of Hercules.* Fotobusta. BELOW: *Maciste, the Greatest Hero in the World.* Fotobusta.

Belgium is a small country, so it is perhaps fitting that the movie posters from this nation are also small; in fact, at 14 1/2 x 21 inches (with a few variations), they are the smallest of any in the world. I suspect that it is because of their diminutive size that so many Belgian posters have survived. Many of these miniature gems, however, are just as filled with action, color and excitement as the larger works from the surrounding countries.

ABOVE: *The Giants of Rome (Fort Alesia).* **RIGHT:** *Hercules vs. the Mercenaries.* Scenes of the hero being tortured or abused are rare in peplum posters, but here the helpless hero suffers in masochistic excess.

au pays le plus mystérieux du monde

L'amour et la vengeance des ardentes gladiatrices

COSMOPOLIS-FILMS présente

SUSY ANDERSEN   JOE ROBINSON

Régie LEONVIOLA

EASTMANCOLOR

TotalScope

LES GLADIATRICES
DE VROUWELIJKE GLADIATOREN

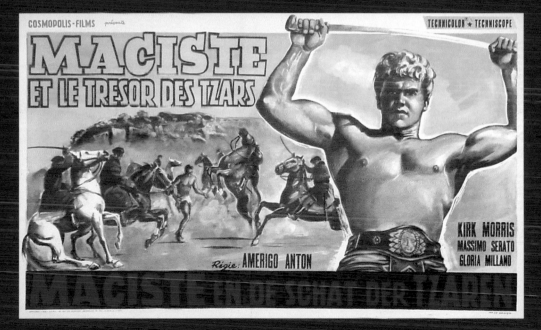

COSMOPOLIS-FILMS présente

TECHNICOLOR ★ TECHNISCOPE

MACISTE
ET LE TRESOR DES TZARS

Régie: AMERIGO ANTON

KIRK MORRIS
MASSIMO SERATO
GLORIA MILLAND

MACISTE EN DE SCHAT DER TZAREN

ABOVE: *The Women Gladiators.* In a wonderful reversal of the usual roles, the shirtless hero remains ineffectively at the sidelines while the girls fight it out. TOP RIGHT: Kirk Morris was one of the handsomest men to play in the peplums. Despite his ruggedly Anglo-Saxon name, he was actually born Adriano Bellini. RIGHT: *Maciste and the Treasure of the Czar.*

ALAN STEEL
MIMMO PALMARA
PILAR CANSINO
JOSE GRECI
ETTORE MANNI

EASTMANCOLOR
TOTALSCOPE

IER MASQUÉ
SKERDE RUITER

ABOVE TOP: *Maciste vs. the Men of Stone.* ABOVE: *The Gladiator of Rome.* LEFT: *Goliath and the Masked Cavalier.* A brilliant and dramatic image compacted into a small space.

LEFT: *The Loves of Hercules.* Jayne Mansfield's monumental mamaries are contrasted with husband, Mickey Hargitay's muscular and aggressive pose.
BELOW LEFT: *Maciste vs. the Monsters.*
BELOW RIGHT: Muscle movie star Mickey Hargitay relaxes with wife Jayne Mansfield and daughter.

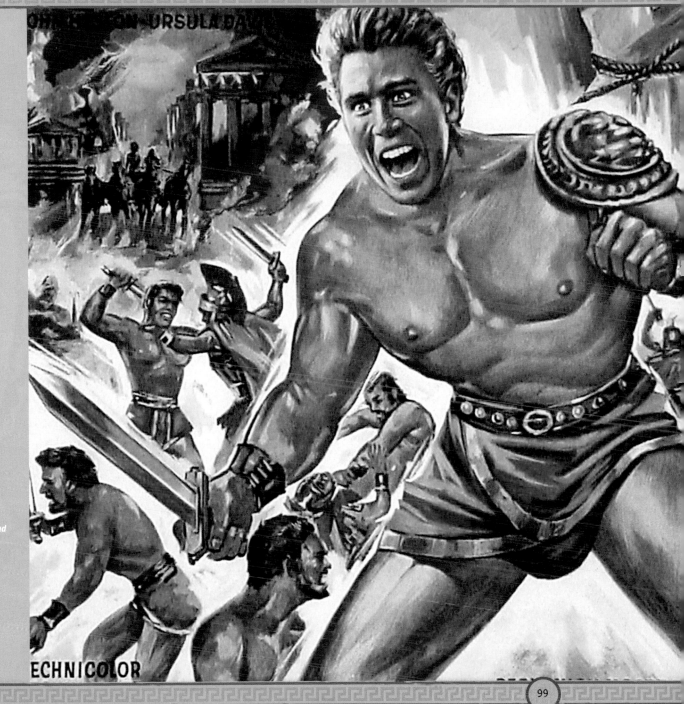

RIGHT: *Spartacus and the Ten Gladiators.*

TOP LEFT: *Maciste in Hell*, original artwork. RIGHT: *The Giant of the Valley of Kings*. Mark Forest (formerly Lou Degni) was an American body-builder of Italian extraction who came to Italy to make peplums.

TOP RIGHT: Goliath and the Conquest of Baghdad. LEFT: *The Vengeance of the Gladiators*. Former Mr. Universe, Mickey Hargitay's physique is clearly the star in this poster.

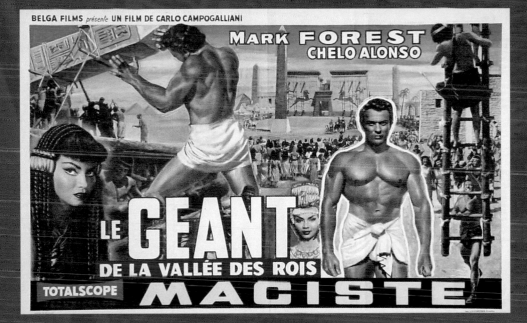

ABOVE: *The Ten Gladiators*, original artwork. Considering the amount of information Belgian posters had to convey, it is a wonder the designs were not more cluttered. Announcing the film in both French and Flemish was difficult enough, but attempting to convey a bit of the plot was even more challenging.

RIGHT: *The Giant of the Valley of Kings*. Mark Forest (formerly Lou Degni) was an American bodybuilder of Italian extraction who came to Italy to make peplums. He had one of the finest physiques in the business, and it is shown very effectively in this poster.

ABOVE: *The Vengeance of Spartacus.*

TOP RIGHT: *Hercules Unchained.*

RIGHT: *Antinea: Hercules and the Conquest of Atlantis.* Poor Reg Park has to take a backseat to the evil queen of Atlantis. Not even Hercules could compete with her big hair and mid-century, swoopy tiara.

ABOVE: *Maciste and the Queen of Troy*. Even two-color posters could be effective if the artwork was good enough. MIDDLE: *The Return of the Titans*. RIGHT: *Maciste, the Strongest Man in the World.*

MARK FOREST

HERCULE CONTRE LES FILS DU SOLEIL

EASTMANCOLOR·SCOPE

avec **ANNA MARIA PAGE**
GIULIANO GEMMA

Mise en scene **OSVALDO CIVIRANI**

HERKULES TEGEN DE ZONEN VAN DE ZON

ABOVE: *Hercules vs. the Sons of the Son.*

LEFT: Mark Forest shows Pharaoh who's boss.

RIGHT: *Maciste vs. the Mongols.*

COSMOPOLIS-FILMS présente

MARK FOREST

José **GRECI**
Ken **CLARK**
Maria-Grazia **SPINA**

MACISTE CONTRE LES MONGOLS

régie D. PAOLELLA

TOTALSCOPE

MACISTE TEGEN DE MONGOLEN

RIGHT: *The Last Days of an Empire.*
BOTTOM LEFT: *Rome in Flames.*
BOTTOM RIGHT: *The Vengeance of Ursus.*

LES ARTISTES ASSOCIÉS S.A.B. présentent

Rosanna
SCHIAFFINO
Bob
MATHIAS

THÉSÉE ET LE MINOTAURE

Alberto LUPO · Rick BATTAGLIA · *"WARLORD OF CRETE"*

TOTALSCOPE

ABOVE: Peplum star Rock Stevens became better known to TV viewers as Peter Lupus in the *Mission Impossible* series. Here he appears in *Hercules vs. the Tyrants of Babylon.* TOP RIGHT: *Theseus and the Minotaur.* RIGHT: *Death in the Arena.*

CENTRA-FILMS présente

MORT DANS L'ARÈNE

TECHNICOLOR
TOTALSCOPE

Régie
Michèle LUPO

MARK FOREST

Scilla GABEL · John CHEVRON
José GRECI · Erno CRISA

DOOD IN DE ARENA

Ein farbenprächtiges Abenteuer voll Spannung und Sensation!

SAMSON UND DER SCHATZ DER INKAS

mit Alan Steel · Toni Sailer
Wolfgang Lukschy · Brigitte Heiberg
Harry Riebauer · Anna Maria Polani u.v.a.

Regie: Piero Pierotti
EIN FARBFILM
Der Constantin-Film-Constantin verleiht im Verleih Constantin-Film

Bold, modern design usually characterizes German peplum posters. Their striking visual appeal is perhaps in compensation for their rather modest size (23 1/2 x 33 1/2 inches).

ABOVE: *Samson and the Treasure of the Incas.* Peplum meets the western in this extraordinary pastiche. RIGHT: Mark Forest is about to be tortured in *Goliath and the Sins of Babylon.*

ABOVE: *Goliath and Hercules.* MIDDLE: *Maciste and the Queen of the Night.*

RIGHT: *Vampire vs. Hercules.* This amazing work breaks all the rules of peplum

posters, yet it perfectly sets the mood for the film. Hercules' powerful fist grasps a

skeletal hand while blood drips from the strongman's chest wound.

ABOVE: *Marco the Invincible.* Saving damsels from a hideous end is more in line with the genre, and this poster does its job admirably. MIDDLE: *Hero from Attica.* RIGHT: *Popaea: The Empress of the Gladiators.*

MARK FOREST

Die Höllenhunde
des
DSCHINGIS KHAN

JOSE' GRECI · KEN CLARK · MARIA G. SPINA · NADIR BALTIMORE · RENATO ROSSINI
Regie: D. PAOLELLA · EASTMANCOLOR · TOTALSCOPE · Produktion: JONIA FILM S.R.L. ROM

DER
UNTERGANG
VON
METROPOLIS

GORDON MITCHELL, BELLA CORTEZ
ROLDANO LUPI, LIANA ORFEI
Regie: Umberto Scarpelli
CERES   Eine CENTRO Produktion in EASTMANCOLOR

SPARTACUS

ABOVE: *The Downfall of Metropolis*. Peplum meets science fiction in this continuation of the famous 1927 silent film by Fritz Lang. MIDDLE: *The Hellhounds of Genghis Khan*. RIGHT: *Spartacus*. It is difficult to think of this poster in any theater, but apparently its overt homoeroticism was either overlooked or accepted by the German public. It is certainly a work of great power and beauty. Needless to say, in the scene on which this was based in the film, both men are clothed.

RIGHT: *Hercules, the Avenger from Rome.* The portrait of Hercules in this poster certainly does not resemble the star, Alan Steel, but the illustration is unquestionably exciting.
BELOW: *Brenno, the Lord of Terror.*

ABOVE: *Theseus, the Hero from Hellas.* Olympic decathlon champion Bob Mathias is given second billing and a background position. A nicely décolleté image of Adriana Rosanna Schiaffino is clearly the principal draw here. MIDDLE: *Battle of the Gladiators.* RIGHT: *The Tribune of Rome,* cover of program booklet.

METROPOLIS - GEHEIMNIS EINER SAGENUMWOBENEN STADT

Der todesmutige Mammutkampf eines mächtigen Reiches gegen die zerschmetternde Kraft gigantischer Naturgewalten

DER UNTERGANG EINER RÄTSELVOLLEN WELT

GORDON MITCHELL in

BELLA CORTEZ · ROLDANO LUPI · LIANA ORFEI · FURIO MENICONI

Regie: UMBERTO SCARPELLI

Eine Centro-Produktion in Eastmancolor

CERES FILM VERLEIH

ABOVE: *The Downfall of Metropolis.* Two-sheet.

GREAT BRITAIN

Sword-and-sandal movies were just as popular in the United Kingdom as they were elsewhere. In order to lure in the customers, the horizontal shaped British "quad" (30 1/2 x 40) was posted at cinemas throughout the island. These posters are generally characterized by busy, crowded designs and bold, primary colors.

ABOVE: Reg Park was born in Leeds in the English Midlands, and he was the only British actor to achieve international fame in peplum films. Here, he poses in a suitably noble attitude.

RIGHT: *Hercules Conquers Atlantis.* One of the few examples of innovative design in British peplum posters. Here, all we see is the hero's massive latisimus dorsi as he stops a runaway chariot.

RIGHT: *Goliath against the Giants.*

BOTTOM LEFT: *Blood of the Warriors.*

BOTTOM RIGHT: *Sons of Thunder.*

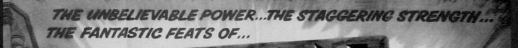

THE UNBELIEVABLE POWER...THE STAGGERING STRENGTH...
THE FANTASTIC FEATS OF...

SAMSON

STARRING
THE STRONGEST
ATHLETE
IN THE WORLD

BRAD HARRIS

WALTER REEVES
BRIGITTE COREY
MARA BERNI
ALAN STEEL

EASTMAN COLOUR   SuperTotalscope

A COMPTON-CAMEO FILMS RELEASE

LEFT: *Samson*. Poor printing, cluttered design, and exaggerated colors that made it look as if the heroes were wearing lipstick were all marks of many English posters. BOTTOM LEFT: Reg Park and co-star Fay Spain commune peacefully. BOTTOM RIGHT: Reg Park and friend clown around on the set at Cinecittà. One of the reasons Park became so popular with audiences is that he cultivated a certain self-mocking quality that went down well with his fans.

MEXICO

BOTTOM LEFT: *Maciste, Son of Goliath.*

BOTTOM RIGHT: *Ulysses vs. Hercules.*

Although they occasionally used larger posters, Mexicans in the 1960s preferred to learn about peplum films from lobby cards. These were slightly larger than the American varieties, but they were much more colorful— some might say, gaudy. Stills from the motion picture are framed by exciting designs that would lure customers to the cinemas.

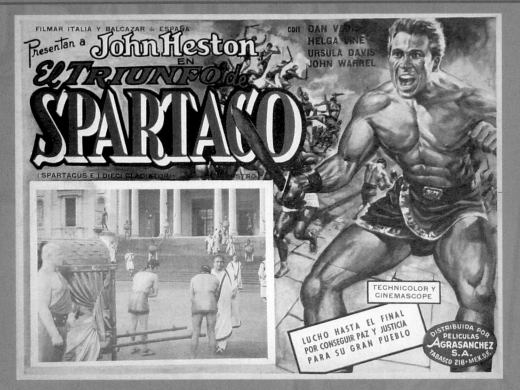

LEFT: *The Triumph of Spartacus*

BOTTOM LEFT: *Ursus.* Crude illustrations of a bullfighter (a natural in Mexico) mark this bold advertisement. BOTTOM RIGHT: *Brenno, Enemy of Rome.* One of the finest portrait illustrations of any Mexican lobby card.

RIGHT: *Maciste vs. the Monsters*. Reg Lewis prepares to bonk a monster on the cabeza. BOTTOM LEFT: *The Strongest Man in the World*. It would be hard to find a poster that did not "read" as well as this one. A muscular hero saves two companions from a gory demise by a cruel machine of death. It's pure peplum. BOTTOM RIGHT: *The Gladiator of Rome*.

LEFT: *Hercules vs. Rome.*
BOTTOM LEFT: *Hercules,*
Samson and Ulysses.
BOTTOM RIGHT: *The*
Vengeance of Ursus.
Gaudily colored Samson
Burke makes short work
of his adversary.

Artistry and visual stimulation are both apparent in Spanish peplum posters. Many of these posters were used throughout the Hispanic world, so they had to communicate to many cultures. Their brilliant designs often belie their relatively modest size: 27 1/2 x 39 1/4 inches.

ABOVE: *Taur, King of Brute Strength.* RIGHT: *The Adventures of Hercules,* lobby card. Mickey Hargitay and wife Jayne Mansfield star in this classic of kitsch. Thanks to a couple of wigs, Mansfield plays both the good and the bad girl. In this scene, Hercules smooches the evil Numaya.

ABOVE: *The Giants of Rome*. Warm, Mediterranean colors accentuate the hero's body in this work. MIDDLE: *The Titans*. RIGHT: *The Triumph of Hercules*. Skillful use of a silhouette adds to the drama of this excellent poster.

LEFT: *The Adventures of Hercules,* lobby card. Hargitay vanquishes one of the silliest monsters ever conceived.

BOTTOM LEFT: *Maciste vs. the Monsters* 1957.

BELOW: *The Trojan War.*

LAS AVENTURAS DE
HERCULES

JAYNE MANSFIELD
MICKEY HARGITAY
MASSIMO SERATO

COLOR

DIRECTOR: C. L. BRAGAGLIA

ALAN **STEEL**
RED **LEWIS**
MARGARET **LEE**

MACISTE CONTRA LOS MONSTRUOS

DIRECTOR
GUIDO MALATESTA
TECHNICOLOR

STEVE REEVES

LA GUERRA DE TROYA

JOHN DREW BARRYMORE • JULIETTE MAYNIEL • HEDY VESSEL
Dirigida por GEORGE FERRONI
SCOPE • EASTMANCOLOR

TURKEY

ABOVE: Handsome Richard Harrison flexes his muscles for two fans. MIDDLE: *The Invincible Three.* A bold design of three upwardly pointing swords contrasted with a vignette of a helpless couple. RIGHT: *The Hero and the Queen.* This is the Turkish version of *Hercules Unchained,* but one would never know it from the illustration.

Bright colors and bold, naive designs characterize the Turkish approach to sword-and-sandal films. Accurate representations of the principal actors are apparently not a priority with some of the artists.

ABOVE: *Nero and the Burning of Rome.* A colorful but crudely limned strongman rescues the requisite helpless damsel. MIDDLE: *Maciste in Pharaoh's Palace.* Once again, the hero's muscular body is displayed in the chain-pull device.

RIGHT: *Revolt of the Gladiators.*

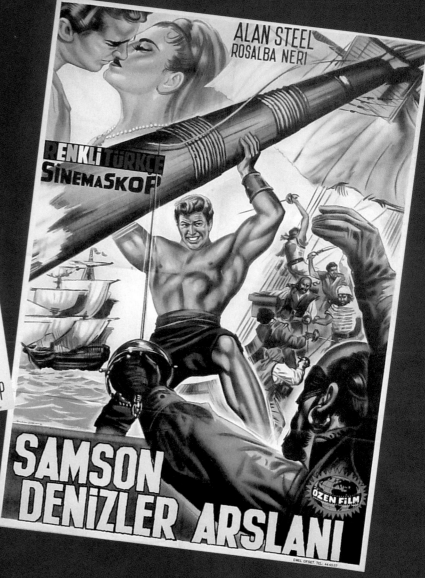

ABOVE: *Hercules vs. the Monster.* RIGHT: *Samson, Lion of the Seas.*

OPPOSITE: *Immortal Gladiator.*

ENDNOTES

1. The best explanation of the term's history and development is found in Aziza, Claude, "Le mot et la chose" in *CinémAction no. 89: Le péplum: l'Antiquité au cinéma* (Courbevoie Éditions Corlet/Télérama, 1998), 7–11.

2. Unfortunately, the reality may be somewhat less spectacular. According to physique photographer Tony Lanza, Francisi saw a photo that the Italian-Canadian camera man had taken in 1947, and sent for Reeves based on that evidence. Interview with Tony Lanza. Montréal, July 31, 2001.

3. The information about the marketing techniques and their results was found in Patrick Lucanio, *With Fire and Sword: Italian Spectacles on American Screens 1858–1968* (Metuchen, N.J.: Scarecrow Press, 1994), 12–13.

4. The character of Maciste has often been linked to the rise of Fascism in Italy. Pagano's countrymen obviously yearned for a benevolent strongman who could set right the wrongs brought about by the Great Depression and a corrupt government. More than one critic has commented on the striking resemblance between Mussolini and Maciste, and this similarity was apparently clear to just about everyone. Pagano's final film appearance was in the Howard Hawks film *Only Angels Have Wings* where the elderly strongman is seen in the background strumming a guitar and singing a song. When this film was first shown in France in May of 1939, the scene was booed because of the actor's resemblance to Il Duce. Quoted in Michel Éloy "Maciste, héros mytho-logique?" in the French Fanzine Maciste (Monster bis: n.p., n.d.), 8.

   For an excellent analysis of the earliest Italian Greco-Roman epics, see Mario Verdone, *Il film atletico e acrobatico* (Torino: Quaderni di documentazione cinematografica, Instituto de Cinema, 1960). This little booklet also contains an excellent filmography of Maciste and his competitors.

5. Quoted in "L'art de l'affiche de cinéma à la française," Bibliothèque du film - Ciné-Regards - Regard sur les collections (www.proto.bifi.fr/cineregards/regard.asp?revue_ref=11). M. Monnier spoke at the inauguration of the first exhibition dedicated to movie posters curated by Henri Langlois at the Cinémathèque française.

6. The title of this film is itself hopelessly exploitative. There are no "captive women" anywhere in the movie.

7. These sexual teases might also have been important to allay the self-doubts and fears of homoeroticism of the audiences. Straight American men have always been concerned about compromises to their masculinity and worries about their sexuality. This would explain not only the reassuringly heterosexual imagery of peplum posters but also swimsuit issues of sports and bodybuilding magazines.

8. The gladius, or short sword, from which the gladiator gets his name was commonly used in Roman times as a humorous synonym for the male member.

9. Jon Solomon, *The Ancient World in the Cinema* (New Haven: Yale University Press, 2001), 313.

10. One critic has detected three categories for women in sword-and-sandal films. "The heroines of the peplums were generally evil queens with hints of lesbianism attached to them; meek, blond 'companions' of the hero; or angry warriors quick to get riled." Francesco La Vitola, *Breve storia della mitologia nel cinema* (Castrovillari: Ecofutura, 1998) 98.

11. Kate Horton, "Luca Brazzi Sleeps with the Fishes: Vendetta and the Ritualized Revenge Motif in Popular Italian Film," in *Queen's University Film Studies*, March 1998, 2. (www.film.queensu.ca/Critical/Horton.html). This article also contains an excellent definition of the Italian filone.

12. Lucanio. in note 17, 10–11.

13. Although *Hercules* was the first modern film in the genre, it represented actually a rebirth. The first series of films set in ancient times occurred at the very beginnings of Italian cinema with films such as *Quo Vadis?* and *Spartacus* in 1913 and the much more famous *Cabiria* a year later. For a fuller explanation and an excellent filmography, see Alberto Farassino and Tatti Sanguinetti (eds), *Gli Uomini Forti* (Milano: Mazzotta, 1983).

14. Two excellent works that deal with the issue of male beauty and concepts of masculinity in film are Gaylyn Studlar, *This Mad Masquerade: Stardom and Masculinity in the Jazz Age* (New York: Columbia University Press, 1996) and Steven Cohan, *Masked Men: Masculinity and the Movies in the Fifties* (Bloomington: Indiana University Press, 1997).

15. All of these hearty, masculine names are noms de cinéma for Edmund Holovchik, Lou Degni, Peter Lupus, Gordon Werschkil, and Sam Berg respectively.

16. There were a very few exceptions to the Anglo-Saxon nomenclature: Jacques Sernas, Enzo Cerusico, Carl Möhner, Pierre Brasseur, and Henri Vidal all presumably kept their own names. Significantly, none of the men in the list hit the big time.